T0345741

THREE EUROPEAN POETS

Three European Poets
Paul Durcan

A collaboration between the
THE IRELAND CHAIR OF POETRY
and

UNIVERSITY COLLEGE DUBLIN PRESS
Preas Choláiste Ollscoile Bhaile Átha Cliath
2017

First published 2017
UNIVERSITY COLLEGE DUBLIN PRESS
UCD Humanities Institute
Room H103
Belfield
Dublin 4
www.ucdpress.ie

These lectures were originally published in *The Poet's Chair: The First Nine Years of the Ireland Chair of Poetry* (The Lilliput Press, 2008), and are reproduced by kind permission of the publisher.

Extracts from Anthony Cronin, *The End of the Modern World*, from *Collected Poems* (New Island, 2004) are reproduced by kind permission of the publisher.

ISBN 978-1-910820-18-6
ISSN 2009-8065 The Poet's Chair Series

CIP data available from the British Library

The right of Paul Durcan to be identified as the author of this work has been asserted by him

Typeset in Adobe Kepler by Ryan Shiels
Text design by Lyn Davies Design
Printed and bound by CPI Group (UK) Ltd, Croydon, CR0 4YY

Contents

FOREWORD

The Trustees of the Ireland Chair of Poetry, in collaboration with UCD Press, are delighted to republish the lectures of Paul Durcan in this handsome volume. The annual lectures of the first three distinguished poets to hold the Chair, John Montague, Nuala Ní Dhomhnaill and Paul Durcan, were originally published in a joint volume, *The Poet's Chair*, by The Lilliput Press in 2008. Since then, UCD Press, in their Writings from the Ireland Chair of Poetry series, has published the lectures of the three eminent poets who subsequently held the Chair: Michael Longley, Harry Clifton and Paula Meehan. This series of individual volumes is now being enhanced with the republication of the lectures of the first three professors; we are most grateful to The Lilliput Press for their immediate consent and their help with this project.

The Ireland Chair of Poetry was established to honour Seamus Heaney's Nobel Prize for Literature in 1995. Modelled on the Oxford Chair of Poetry which Seamus held with grace and distinction, the Ireland Chair is a cross-border collaboration involving the two Irish Arts Councils, north and south, Queen's University Belfast, Trinity College Dublin and University College Dublin. A highlight of the professorship is the annual public lecture each professor gives and their publication constitutes an important record of the poets' engagement with their own work and that of other poets. Each of them has carried on a noble tradition of sharing their learning with new generations.

As Donnell Deeny noted in his preface to the original publication of these lectures, Paul Durcan's 'voice in Irish poetry has been unique and carrying, his body of work remarkable. Paul has, with his scholarly lectures and successful engagement with all three universities, emphasized his ability as a critic of signal originality, having already shown himself a skilled broadcaster and prose writer.' In these lectures, Paul Durcan celebrates works by three important fellow-poets with a rigorous and detailed analysis that is masterful and wide-ranging.

Our sincere thanks to Mary Clayton who worked tirelessly to bring this project to fruition. I must also thank all of my other fellow Trustees, both former and currently serving, ably supported by administrator Niamh McCabe. The Ireland Chair of Poetry Trust has an assured future because of their commitment and I know that each one of them would say, with me, that it is an honour to be associated with such a visionary project.

SHEILA PRATSCHKE
Chair of the Board of Trustees, Ireland Chair of Poetry
September 2017

Cronin's Cantos

We went to Brighton in our Little Nine,
The open touring model Leslie bought
On what was called H.P. A gorgeous day,
The sky was somehow deep, you know, like heaven,
I thought the bubbling tar might melt the tyres
And Leslie laughed, called me a silly juggins.
He was a lovely driver, doing forty
Once we were free of Staines. It's tommy rot
To tell us now that people weren't happy.
We had our own nice house, a tudor villa,
Which was the new thing then, a vacuum cleaner,
Dance music on the wireless, lovely murders.
Of course the war was still to come, that Hitler,
But it all seemed somehow new then, somehow modern.

[Sonnet 95]

In literary Dublin in the early winter months of 1963 – for there did exist then such a blood-and-guts encampment as 'literary Dublin' (it has of course long vanished from the River Liffey's banks) – there were rumours and whispers concerning the possibly imminent return to Dublin from Spain of a man called Cronin. Literary Dublin encompassed a small slope, running up from the Liffey on the north shore of Trinity College to the Grand Canal on the south shore of University College. At night in the pubs around the camp fires, mutterings and speculation, innuendo and foreboding went on about this man called Cronin.

All that winter, it was always night; I remember no daylight. Personages were as much shadows as substances, and you could as much intimate them as discern them. Patrick Kavanagh, John Jordan, James Liddy and Harry Kernoff were in McDaids, Brendan Behan and John Ryan were in the Bailey, Sean O'Sullivan was in Neary's, Ronnie Drew and Luke Kelly were in O'Donoghues, Leland Bardwell was in O'Dwyers, Macdara Woods was in Bartley Dunnes, Michael Longley and Derek Mahon and Brendan Kennelly were in O'Neills, and Michael Hartnett and myself were everywhere.

Has Cronin arrived?
He has.
He has not.

I was eighteen years old, setting out on the road to be a poet and nothing but a poet, so help me Dostoyevsky. I had spent my adolescent years reading up about Moscow and now I had set foot on the road to Moscow. Little did I know, in no way could I have foreseen, that that was how I would spend the rest of my life, tramping the road to Moscow. I could not figure out at all clearly why this Cronin man was the cause of such apprehension and expectation. Some said that he was a Communist. Others that he was a poet. He was a tyrant, an upstart, a saint, a genius. The wet dark nights were rife with suspense. What would he look like, I wondered, this intellectual pirate who was about to swoop in from the sea? I thought I had read every contemporary Irish poet and yet I had never seen, much less read a line by Cronin. I felt like Jack Hawkins in The Admiral Benbow waiting on the cliffs to catch sight of the figurehead of the schooner of doom or ecstasy, salvation or damnation, Dr Livesey invisible at my shoulder.

And then he was there. He was here. Six feet away from me. At midnight in the basement flat of Leland Bardwell. 33 Lower Leeson Street. Amongst the writers and the ex-revolutionaries and all the rest of the Bohemian flotsam and jetsam with their brown bags of stout and the odd naggin of whiskey. I didn't have to be told it was Cronin. In dress

and style as well as in person, he was completely different from every-
one else in that dungeon. A slight, dark, handsome man of about forty
and middle height. Spanish-looking. His slightly pugilistic, slightly
amatory posture was as if he had just stepped out the stage door at the
back of the bullfight arena. Norman Mailer disguised as El Cordobés. A
light corduroy suit, white shirt and tie, black beret, a cigarette in one
hand, a bottle in the other, conversing fiercely with those nearest to
him, conducting life-and-death arguments, yet suddenly collapsing in
mirth, only to rise and sink the *banderilla* into his neighbour's shoul-
der blade. Politics, history, poetry, war, horse racing, boxing, Liberty,
Equality, Fraternity; and Injustice.

In the weeks and months that followed over the next two years I
was to find myself often in the company of Anthony Cronin. Naturally I
was never introduced to him. I was a boy of eighteen on the edge of the
crowd but it seemed to me that he treated me as he treated everyone
else – as an equal companion. Angry, impatient, idealistic intellectual
he was, but equally he was gentle. What the young e. e. cummings
wrote about walking Paris streets at night with the older Ezra Pound
would also be true of how I perceived Cronin in the early 1960s: 'He was
more than wonderfully entertaining: he was magically gentle as only a
great man can be towards some shyest child.' He was all soft edge as
well as all hard edge. He had phenomenal memory, wit, knowledge and
sense. And always, then as now, forty-two years later, that hovering
glint of a smile and that shingle beach intake of breath prefiguring a
three-stroke chuckle as he awaited his moment to expose the cant the
rest of us were regurgitating. He had as rigorous and subtle a critical
mind as T. S. Eliot but as audacious a footstep as Ezra Pound. Twenty
years later in 1984, the legendary Steward of Annaghmakerrig, Bernard
Loughlin, employed one word to describe Cronin: 'cniptious'.

A typical ordinary spring evening in 1963 comes to mind. It is about
five in the afternoon in O'Dwyers public house on the corner of Lower
Leeson Street and St Stephen's Green. Cronin is sitting with his back to
the frosted glass with a review copy of a new Alan Sillitoe novel on his
lap. He is reviewing it for the *TLS*. This is how Cronin makes his living:

book-reviewing and most other forms of hack journalism. I have never met such a creature before. A fully qualified, fully harassed member of Grub Street. His glamorous, yellow-haired Mayo wife Thérèse is sitting beside him checking and sorting out other review books to help her husband. Out of the blue, Cronin quotes the American poet Hart Crane, the greatest American modernist poet of them all: a passage from the hobo section of Crane's epic poem *The Bridge*. Cronin utters the lines with a mixture of joy and outrage and laughter as if he were Danton or Baudelaire at the bar of the French Chamber of Deputies:

> Behind
> My father's cannery works I used to see
> Rail-squatters ranged in nomad raillery,
> The ancient men – wifeless or runaway
> Hobo-trekkers that forever search
> An empire wilderness of freight and rails.
> Each seemed a child, like me, on a loose perch,
> Holding to childhood like some termless play.
> John, Jake or Charley, hopping the slow freight
> – Memphis to Tallahassee – riding the rods,
> Blind fists of nothing, humpty-dumpty clods.
>
> Yet they touch something like a key perhaps.
> From pole to pole across the hills, the states
> – They know a body under the wide rain;
> Youngsters with eyes like fjords, old reprobates
> With racetrack jargon, – dotting immensity
> They lurk across her, knowing her yonder breast
> Snow-silvered, sumac-stained or smoky blue –
> Is past the valley-sleepers, south or west.
> – As I have trod the rumorous midnights, too,
>
> And past the circuit of the lamp's thin flame
> (O Nights that brought me to her body bare!)
> Have dreamed beyond the print that bound her name.

[4]

Trains sounding the long blizzards out – I heard
Wail into distances I knew were hers.
Papooses crying on the wind's long mane
Screamed redskin dynasties that fled the brain,
– Dead echoes! But I knew her body there,
Time like a serpent down her shoulder, dark,
And space, an eaglet's wing, laid on her hair.

['The River']

Cronin then relates the story of Hart Crane's suicide and how just
before he leapt from the stern of the *SS Orizaba* another passenger asked
Crane how he was feeling and Hart replied: 'Like a rat in a trap'. This
leads into a story about David Gascoyne visiting Herne Cottage in Sussex
near Tennyson's house where the Cronins had lived in the 1950s. From
Gascoyne, on then to George Barker and suddenly to John Cornford.
Silence. Grief. The Spanish Civil War. Killed at twenty-one during the
second battle of the Ebro. Cornford's poem to his girl back in England,
Margot Heinemann. Cronin throws back his head defiantly and quotes
the poem by heart again, by heart. All of it, all of it:

Heart of the heartless world,
Dear heart, the thought of you
Is the pain at my side,
The shadow that chills my view.

The wind rises in the evening,
Reminds that autumn is near,
I am afraid to lose you,
I am afraid of my fear.

On the last mile to Huesca,
The last fence for our pride,
Think so kindly, dear, that I
Sense you at my side.

[5]

And if bad luck should lay my strength
Into the shallow grave,
Remember all the good you can;
Don't forget my love.

['Huesca']

Shillings, sixpences and three-penny bits are counted to procure a few
more beers and someone mentions President John F. Kennedy who is
due to fly into Dublin in a month or two whereupon Cronin names a
name no one has ever heard of – Robert Duncan – and he begins to
sing:

Hoover, Roosevelt, Truman, Eisenhower –
where among these did the power reside
that moves the heart? What flower of the nation
bride-sweet broke to the whole rapture?
Hoover, Coolidge, Harding, Wilson
hear the factories of human misery turning out commodities.
For whom are the holy matins of the heart ringing?
Noble men in the quiet of morning hear
Indians singing the continent's violent requiem.
Harding, Wilson, Taft, Roosevelt,
idiots fumbling at the bride's door,
hear the cries of men in meaningless debt and war.
Where among these did the spirit reside
that restores the land to productive order?

['A Poem Beginning with a Line by Pindar']

That was just an ordinary spring evening in O'Dwyers public house in
the month of April 1963. And those of us who were lucky enough to be
sitting there were being vouchsafed a rare kind of education. Cronin in
O'Dwyers in the early 1960s was the classic Central European artist-
intellectual and hedge schoolmaster practising Newman's idea of a
university in the corner of a smoky bar. Cronin set me free. After

Kavanagh, he put the final kybosh on the curse of flag-waving, tattooed Celtic poetry, fairies, wet turf and the treble-whammy whine of self-pity, retrophilia, and nostalgia.

Another evening in 1963, a summer's evening, Cronin is sitting on the far side of O'Dwyers lounge bar, at least six or seven people around him when I enter. I sit on the edge and listen to Cronin debate with a young man from Lurgan, County Armagh called Michael Deeny (later in life to be manager of Horslips and a financial wizard in the City of London) the pros and cons of the Franco-Prussian war of 1870. Young Deeny puts up a brave, spectacular show but Cronin's mastery of detailed fact and his eloquence would have trounced Socrates and he would have given A. J. P. Taylor a serious run for his money. It was evident that for Cronin there were no neat frontiers between work and leisure, poetry and history and philosophy and economics and art. He was mixing them all the time but fundamentally from a poet's point of view. To purify my metaphor, he was Norman Mailer disguised as Cassius Clay.

This was what made the poet Cronin different from any other poet in Ireland: his ferocious passion for ideas. Back then in 1963 and ever since. Ideas for Cronin were as much flesh and blood as sex. And now forty-two years later I can say that I have met only one other Irish writer of whom I could say the same in respect of the intellect being as visceral as the heart and that is John Moriarty and, amazingly and wonderfully, two more different artist-intellectuals you could not meet than Cronin and Moriarty. Polar opposites joined at the equatorial conscience by passion for thought and language that admits absolutely no compromise.

But still I had not read a line by Cronin. His one collection of poems entitled *Poems*, published in London by The Cresset Press in 1958, was out of print and unobtainable. It would not be until a long two years later and David Wright's Penguin anthology of poetry, *The Mid-Century*, published in 1965, that I or anyone of my generation would have revealed to us what a new and outstanding poet Cronin was. With what excitement of raw recognition I read Cronin's *Lines for a Painter*, *Elegy for the Nightbound*, and *Responsibilities*. In the following year, 1966, Penguin published Wright's companion anthology of *Longer Contemporary*

Poems, in which alongside W. H. Auden's *Letter to Lord Byron*, Hugh MacDiarmid's *On a Raised Beach*, W. S. Graham's *The Nightfishing*, Patrick Kavanagh's *The Great Hunger*, I read Anthony Cronin's *RMS Titanic* and realised the huge, world-stage poetic stature of the man. Journalist, broadcaster, reviewer, controversialist, intellectual, activist, he was most certainly all of these; but never again would I mistake him for being anything other than that rare specimen, the original, radical, unique, uncompromisable poet. What set Cronin apart was his absolutely uncompromising commitment to honesty in his writing as well as in his person, no matter what the cost.

Twenty years later, in February 1983, I found myself in snow-dumped, blizzard-blazing Moscow – the actual city in Russia in old Soviet Union time under Andropov – in the company of Anthony Cronin. I noticed again and again the shock on the faces of Party *apparatchiks* at the fact that Cronin was so much more obviously a true *tovarich* than any of themselves. Secondly, I recall the hardest and profoundest lesson I have ever received in the art of poetry. Sitting in the window seat of an Aeroflot airliner flying across the mountain peaks of the Caucasus from Armenia back to Moscow I remarked to Cronin who was in the aisle seat that the peaks below 'look like tents'. Cronin, with the stern, anxious, exasperated expression of a parent whose patience has been tested to the limit, remonstrated with me. 'Paul, will you please stop saying that things are *like* things. Either they *are* or they *are not*.'

In the snows of the Soviet Union in the winter of 1983, Cronin the Marxist idealist poet as plain and casual in his mode of dress as in his speech – a windcheater, a jumper, a cloth cap – was about as much out of place among the new generation of decadent Party men and the new Gorbachev reformers as a veteran of the 1917 revolution would have been: one of those veterans all of whom Stalin exterminated in the 1930s. In the Party rooms in Moscow in the winter of 1983 Cronin shone in the darkness like a brother of the radiant Bukharin.

Max Eastman wrote of meeting them on trains
When under Lenin's leadership the country
Was just emerging from the Civil War.

Middle-aged men with philosophic foreheads,
Motherly, grey-haired women with calm eyes,
A younger woman, sensuous, beautiful.
Who bore herself as if she had once walked
Up to a cannon's mouth. You would enquire,
He said, and you would find these were the veterans,
Taught in infancy to love mankind,
Master themselves, be free from sentiment,
The high traditions of the terrorist movement.
They had learned in youth a new mode from the party,
To think in practical terms, was how he put it.

[Sonnet 149]

The second of April 1989 was a mild, calm, stationary spring day in
Dublin. It was a Sunday, and just a little after eight o'clock in the day-
light of eventide, a sixty-four-year-old poet began to read from a new
book. There was a full but not complete audience in the function room
of Buswell's Hotel, a modest Georgian inn, which stands opposite the
gates to the parliament of the Republic of Ireland. Outside, except for
two policemen, the streets were empty. The sort of mundane setting in
which a tumultuous event occurs or a prophet gets born. The poet was
Anthony Cronin and the new book was entitled *The End of the Modern
World*. After the reading, I knew that not since the publication in 1928
of *The Tower* by W. B. Yeats had Irish history known such an occasion.
For in this new book-long poem of 161 sonnets Cronin had taken up the
same intellectual as well as artistic challenge as had his fire-eating pre-
decessor: he had attempted, dared to survey, depict, analyse Western
civilisation from the Middle Ages to the era of the Twin Towers of
Manhattan.

Fifteen years later on 2 November 2004 in another Georgian house
around the corner on the west side of St Stephen's Green on the occasion
of the publication of his *Collected Poems* Anthony Cronin read from his
slightly enlarged, slightly revised version of *The End of the Modern
World*, the number of sonnets having increased from the 161 of 1989 to
179. It was an occasion of momentous gentleness and to my own mind

[9]

came back a memory of the eighty-year-old Ezra Pound's assignation with Mrs George Yeats in 1965 in the Royal Hibernian Hotel in Dawson Street off the north side of the Green. Grace; graceful; gracefully.

A sequence of 179 sonnets is Cronin's preferred designation of *The End of the Modern World*. But with respect I am referring to it, first, as one long poem, all of a piece, and, secondly, as 'Cronin's Cantos'.

In embarking on this enormous long poem, Cronin set himself the same problem as Ezra Pound had set himself during the First World War. How to adumbrate in verse the history of Western civilisation? Pound's solution was to begin an open-ended work-in-progress in free verse called the *Cantos*. Somewhere Pound had written – probably more than once – that the first task of the modern poet was to break the dominance of the iambic pentameter line. But Cronin's solution, astonishingly, was not only to return to the iambic pentameter line but to return to it in its most conventional guise, the sonnet form.

Nor did Cronin choose the strait-jacket of the sonnet as Robert Lowell and John Berryman when they performed ego-manoeuvres and self-regarding monologues of solipsistic erudition and vanity gossip.

I believe that Cronin probably came to his solution via Auden and Kavanagh. In Cronin's early verse you can hear Auden plainly. But the unusual thing about Cronin is that, perhaps by wholly surrendering himself to Auden, he emerged with his own tone of voice intact; that tone of voice that comes off the page at you like no other *modern* Irish poet.

And then there was Kavanagh! In the early 1950s Kavanagh gave Cronin, as he gave anyone who cared to listen, permission to write verse about anything – anything – with the exception of 'Ireland'. 'The Irish Thing' as Kavanagh called it was a dead end, which indeed it was. Instead Kavanagh wrote a sonnet called 'The Hospital' and it's a long way from 'The Hospital' back to 'Bright star, would I were steadfast as thou art'.

> A year ago I fell in love with the functional ward
> Of a chest hospital: square cubicles in a row
> Plain concrete, wash basins – an art lover's woe,

Not counting how the fellow in the next bed snored.
But nothing whatever is by love debarred,
The common and banal her heat can know.
The corridor led to a stairway and below
Was the inexhaustible adventure of a gravelled yard.

This is what love does to things: the Rialto Bridge,
The main gate that was bent by a heavy lorry,
The seat at the back of a shed that was a suntrap.
Naming these things is the love-act and its pledge;
For we must record love's mystery without claptrap,
Snatch out of time the passionate transitory.

['The Hospital']

I imagine that what Cronin discovered in the laboratory of his verse experiments was that Kavanagh's sonnet 'The Hospital' enabled the poet to include anything, no matter how banal, and yet still be in position to strike the singing line, viz, to create his own 'canto'. To me, one of the great achievements and great beauties of *The End of The Modern World* is the juxtaposition of banal prose with the singing line. It's the prose basis of his poetry that makes Cronin's poetry such pure poetry.

But also, by employing the sonnet for his gigantic purpose, Cronin was opening up other possibilities of technical enhancement which have worked out perfectly. The sonnet frees Cronin from having to occupy the false position of narrative. The 179 sonnets as a whole constitute a tour-de-force technical accomplishment of collage technique, montage, intricate patchwork, cinematic editing; snapshots, headlines, quotations, bubbles, captions, slogans, advertisements. Paradoxically, of course, by eschewing narrative through his use of the sonnet, Cronin succeeds in achieving in verse an outstanding feat of storytelling. He tells the story of his own mind's adventures across the mountains and the seas of the history of Western man.

What follows here is a personal account of my sixteen years of reading, reading, reading *The End of the Modern World*. My account is as much about my own pleasure in reading the poem as it is about the poem itself.

As with any outstanding work of art, a Gothic cathedral, a Sibelius symphony, the architecture of Cronin's *The End of the Modern World* in its finished state seems outrageously simple, unbelievably simple. The 179 sonnets are divided into three sections or, musically speaking, three movements. Part I (Sonnets 1–48) begins with the birth of modern farming in the high Middle Ages and feudalism, and concludes with the French Impressionists painting quickly with their women at Argenteuil on the Seine outside Paris on a Sunday afternoon. Along the way the poet introduces his major and minor themes that will recur throughout the other two sections. Early on the poet reports two famous works by Burne-Jones: *The Arming of the Knights,* a drawing in the Birmingham City Art Gallery, and the extraordinary painting, *King Cophetua and the Beggar Maid* in the Tate in London. These two archetypal works epitomise the Male Chivalry Dream or the Male Chivalry Myth of the Ideal Female, which Cronin sees at the heart of both medieval Europe and modern Hollywood. From Galahad to Clark Gable. This myth is a revolving glass in Cronin's mind throughout history as again and again he returns to the question of the relationship of man and woman.

Next, the Birth of Commerce and the Laws of Property and Tort, the sale of land and the concept in the Western world of the 'buyability' of everything.

But even at this early stage of the story nothing is seen in isolation. Good and Evil are inextricable. Cronin composes odes to great progress in architecture in the seventeenth and eighteenth centuries.

Then the first almighty political cataclysm of the modern era – the French Revolution. In one small single sonnet, an exquisite vignette of Cronin and the Italian poet Luciano Erba walking the grounds of the Schloss Leopold at the Salzburg Festival in 1951, discussing the French Revolution:

> But strike they did and threw a king's cropped head
> As gage of battle to the kings of Europe,
> Thus horrifying many gentle souls.
> And Erba said, a far day to remember,

Walking beside Max Reinhardt's urns and columns,
Two suns, the second broken on the water,
Schloss Leopold, the joy of the baroque,
A tracery across the darker side,
No Barbara that day; 'Unhappiness
Came into Europe with that revolution
As mode where only misery had been.'
Through thirty years quite clear, two poets in amber.
Now after all those years I find the answer:
No, not unhappiness but discontent.

[Sonnet 27]

Robert Emmet in three sonnets speaks with a candour not unlike
Cronin's own direct mode of conversation:

'They dragged the Lord Chief Justice from his coach,
A mottled and blanched old man who loved his grandchild.
This has been held against me ever since
Alike by those who say, what is, is right,
And those who say what is not should remain
With unstained annals until it becomes
The true republic, Roman, rational.
My superbly folded stock and flowered waistcoat,
The justice and humanity of my cause,
My acquaintance with the works of Paine and Rousseau,
Worthless, in face of this. Yet this was progress.
Your other sad rebellions had been raised
For rural reasons. Mine at least were modern.
My mob was European, avant-garde.

[Sonnet 30]

Cronin and his comrade Brendan Behan visit the grave of Heine in the
Père Lachaise cemetery in Paris or, rather, *happen* on the grave of
Heine. They 'see' Heine's grave. Cronin is ever faithful to the process of
drift and happenstance in life.

[13]

Cronin exposes the essence of the bourgeois lie of the Western world. Baudelaire understands that the basis of bourgeois civilisation is prostitution:

> The moral order of the bourgeois world,
> Whose basis, as he knew, was prostitution
>
> [Sonnet 44]

And so to Lautrec and La Goulue in the Moulin Rouge and finally to the girls at Argenteuil, concluding Part I:

> Girls on the river, girls at Argenteuil,
> Under the dappling trees in August light,
> Skirts full and creamy like cloth waterfalls
> Brushing the grass, each ankle an example
> Of how athletic angels are, as eager
> They stepped on land at one of Sunday's stages.
> The light declined at last. The dance began
> And music mingled with the wine in veins
> Alive to summer and condemned to Monday.
> Passion like night might follow light's decline
> And be at odds with openness of glance,
> Which should have lasted longer. We could ask
> Was the whole day as easy as it seems,
> Their comradeship unclouded like the moon?
>
> [Sonnet 48]

Part II (Sonnets 49–97) brings us slap right bang back to the beginning of the whole human story – to the Garden of Eden:

> What was it like in the Garden? As naked as birch trees,
> Their skin as native a sight as sheen of the river,
> The curve of buttock but as the curve of bole,
> No cloth occluding its shock or smooth synthetics,
> To cling, suggest, to ruck and to reveal?

[14]

And psyches without disguise or covering either,
Everything natural, instinctive, happy,
No kinks, no hang-ups and no fetishes,
No thought thought daring, or no thought at all.
It may have been a munch, but Baudelaire
Would not have been at home there, nor, in truth,
Might you, O hypocrite lecteur, less hyp–
Ocrite perhaps, more hip than them,
Those clear-eyed innocents in unshadowed groves.

[Sonnet 49]

There follows a generously critical, witty, yet slightly sympathetic account of Milton's lofty nonsense about the Original Item, the First Couple. Here are sonnets of virtuoso urbanity, choc-a-bloc with aphorisms to keep the reader thinking until the bell tolls in the garden and it is time to be whipped out the gates. The sexual question is approached again over a different course, the poles of the fences higher this time round. Freud, de Sade and most especially Ms Angela Carter are responded to:

Knowledge is power, yes, but power is knowledge.

[Sonnet 53]

Or

Of course most women were as ignorant
About themselves as any man could be

[Sonnet 54]

But what is most thrilling of all is the actual writing itself – verse of such an order that the reader is lifted up on the waves of the energy of the poet's absolute fidelity both to his material and to his craft. Wit, humour, romance, verve, lucidity, élan, gusto; he has managed to get all of his own unique conversational, convivial human voice behind the verse and under the verse and in the verse. Sonnet 57, for example, is simply pure poetic statement without any of the frills or evasions or tricks that most poets feel compelled to resort to:

> The lower middle classes still believed
> There never could be much and that much worked for.
> And even the romantics were quite certain
> That money could not buy the things that mattered:
> The steady grey-eyed gaze of understanding,
> Time waiting on a leaf in autumn woods,
> The envied love of enviable women.
> One hardly needs to add that they missed out on
> Much that was merely a short drive away,
> A passing taxi or a routine flight.
> Journey they must if lovers will have meetings.
> Nor do the happy ask when they have landed,
> Why money like the ocean drowns all guilt,
> Why the shore smiles on those who have attained it.
>
> [Sonnet 57]

To that last sonnet as to so much of Cronin's entire project, I would apply Ezra Pound's comment on Ford Madox Ford in Pound's 1914 essay 'The prose tradition in verse': 'I find him significant and revolutionary because of his insistence upon clarity and precision, upon the prose tradition; in brief, upon efficient writing – even in verse.'

There follows a sequence on Vienna before the First World War – that nightmare city of Karl Kraus, Klimt, Schiele, Adolph Loos. Two sonnets on Valentia Island are a prelude to a depiction of Picasso's 1907 painting *Les Demoiselles d'Avignon* from MOMA in New York which is the middle painting of the three crucial paintings of the poem; the first being Burne-Jones's *King Cophetua* and the third near the poem's end being Van Gogh's *The Starry Night* (1889, also in MOMA). Of Picasso's preparatory sketches for *Les Desmoiselles* the critic William Rubin suggests a progression 'from the narrative to the iconic'; the same should be also said of Cronin's poetic technique.

[16]

Enter Lenin, Matisse, Marinetti, Blériot, as well as Picasso. In such close and natural proximity, such a galaxy seems unbearable and it is. The First World War erupts and in Berlin the young historian Friedrich Meinecke bears witness:

> In the summer twilight thousands filled the streets,
> Embracing, weeping, eyes and faces shining.
> And then as darkness fell there came the singing,
> The old heart-breaking songs, the mighty, soaring
> Es braust ein Ruf wie Donnerhall and after
> The stern strong hymn of German Protestants,
> Ein' feste Burg ist unser Gott. I moved
> Slowly along the Wilhelmstrasse with them
> It was as if I floated with the crowds,
> Forgetful now of self, immersed like them
> In a great tide of Germanness, of oneness.
> Although what was to come was terrible
> That night seems still august, magnificent.
> I shiver when I think of it today.

[Sonnet 74]

But at the war front the painter Fernand Léger experiences a total aesthetic liberation finding himself,

> ... among real, intractable things

[Sonnet 77]

Lenin's hysteria, Tatlin's and El Lissitzky's fantastic architectural plans, an ode to the automobile.

And now Cronin plucks out of his magic Bulgakovian handkerchief a snapshot of the painter Picabia of whom Ezra Pound once famously remarked: 'Picabia is the man who ties the knots in Picasso's tail.'

Picabia at the wheel of a Bugatti,
The horn bulb to his painterly right hand,

[Sonnet 86]

We pause for a moment, for one sonnet, to put Romantic Ireland in her place before it's time for another ode to the city, which is pure Audenesque, yet pure Cronin. I estimate Cronin was sixty years old when he composed Sonnet 92; only a poet in his prime could write with such authority, such confidence, all his powers under full sail:

Let the city open tonight, an unfolding flower
Not yet full blown, glass petals tipped with promise,
Let it greet its lovers with wide embracing tracks,
Narrowing nearer to the nervous centre.
Let the neon signs throw roses on shining pavements
As the dusk of summer softens each separate vista.
Let the tigerish hide of the quarter proclaim a fierce
Energy in this decadence, this danger.
Let all be famous, but everyone to be anonymous,
Let all find their old friends, but stalk expectant
Through swathes of faces, seeking the lovely stranger.
Let the wicked streets be happy, the happy ones wicked,
Let us tremble, so great the depravity, lurid the darkness,
But come to the leafy gardens, finding the loved one.

[Sonnet 92]

Part III (Sonnets 98–179) begins in the family quarters of the precise, law-abiding, meticulous family man and Commandant of Auschwitz, Rudolf Höss. We tread the cinder path,

… laid to the door of the officers' quarters
Of cinders cleared from the incinerators.

[Sonnet 102]

From the super-modern efficiency of Auschwitz we go straight to the Royal Festival Hall and the Hayward Gallery on London's South Bank. These are the viral connections of *The End of the Modern World*. It is Cronin's capacity to make such viral connections that lifts his great poem up into the realm of *The Waste Land*. Back once more, more ruthlessly than before, to the sexual question, Angela Carter (author of *The Sadeian Woman*) and D. H. Lawrence.

And then at last we come to one of the very special glories of Cronin's opus: what those of us who have been reading the poem for the last sixteen years call 'the autobiographical sequence' or what Cronin himself in the body of the poem calls 'the Stella Gardens sequence' (Sonnets 116–22). In the heart of the Dublin docklands there is a small redbrick terrace enclave known only to the dock workers of Dublin and it is known as Stella Gardens and there in one of these tiny cottages in the 1970s Cronin with his wife and two young daughters, Iseult and Sarah, made their home. Without a hint of disingenuousness, coyness, false humility, pretentious slumming, mock irony, inverted snobbery or self-pity Cronin contrasts his working-class postage-stamp abode with W. B. Yeats's Tower at Thoor Ballylee:

> There was supposed to be a Stella Gardens sequence
> To put Yeats and his tower in their place,
> For, after all, a visitor I had
> Opined our little quarter had been built
> For the aristocracy of labour – dockers,
> Violent and bitter men perhaps when drinking.
> The master bedroom measured twelve by six,
> The other, square but smaller had no window
> Since someone built the kitchen up against it.
> The loo was out of doors. I don't complain.
> In fact the Stella poems, like extensions
> Projected, never started for the want
> Of money, time and energy, were meant
> To celebrate, as he did, rootedness.

[Sonnet 116]

[19]

Onwards, backwards to the zeitgeist of the 1960s, the eerie funeral of Robert Kennedy, the interior life of Elvis Presley. Only to arrive at Sonnet 131:

O lady of the moon whose profiled face
Halts our walk homeward underneath the trees,
Shine on unblessedness your blessing now,
Wed our desire with our desire to please.
Lonely Actaeon saw your bared, pale flesh
Through celluloid of water, silver bright,
And stood prolonging this unholy joy
Feasting on nerve ends in the moon's limelight.
You turned your back, autogamous as he,
But knew him gazing still on that expanse,
Turning to stasis what should be a dance.
Turning to wrong and sulkiness what should
Have touched with joy that whole nocturnal wood.

Approaching the climacteric of the poem, Cronin offers brutal, poignant depictions of modern England destroyed by Margaret Thatcher, the Russian Revolution and the life and work of Vincent Van Gogh:

And Arthur Scargill in his madness said,
'I see Jehovah in the wintry sun
Which looks to her like any golden guinea.
I see the lamb of god in England's fields.'
And so on a bright day in England's winter
When Trafalgar Square lies dry and sharp and shadowed
We ask the right to work, close punk rock ranks
Beneath the heavy portico behind
Which shelter many splendid works of art
And underneath Lord Nelson who broke rules
But saved the bacon of the ruling class.
More moral than those rulers we reject
A life of idleness, a lack of aim,
Of purpose, effort, patriotic zeal.

[Sonnet 147]

Sonnet 152 begins:

> Childe Roland to the dark tower came ...

We have hit the climacteric of the poem with twenty-two sonnets to go. Who is Childe Roland? Howard Hughes, possibly. Corporate man, certainly. Certes also the man against whom Karl Kraus in Vienna in 1922 in his play *Last Days of Mankind*, had warned; Kraus's thesis being, as summed up by Erich Heller in *The Disinherited Mind* (p. 218): 'Man has achieved a technical superiority over himself which threatens him with unavoidable disaster.' The Dark Tower might be the Hong Kong Stock Exchange or the International Financial Services Centre in Dublin but in the conclusion of Cronin's poem it is located actually in Manhattan. Whew! Bear in mind that these final sonnets were first published in 1989, twelve years before the attack on the Twin Towers. Who leered that poetry was not prophetic?

Childe Roland appears first as the mythical figure in Browning's poem of the same name who, having succeeded in his quest to find the Dark Tower does not enter, but instead, as Browning has him, says:

> And yet
> Dauntless the slug-horn to my lips I set,
> And blew. '*Childe Roland to the Dark Tower came.*'

But Cronin's Childe Roland does not merely come, he penetrates:

> Childe Roland to the dark tower came and climbed
> The massive steps in natural trepidation.
> But when the blonde beyond the blinding fountain
> Asked him his name and business, his composure
> Returned. He coolly showed his new ID
> And obeying bored directions took the bronze
> Lift to the fourteenth floor as he'd been told.
> He smiled quite naturally at them while he noted
> That Evil preferred its girls gaunt, doe-eyed, starving,

And thought it would be nice to get to know
The ones he met, while being quite aware
The person they responded to could never
Be himself. In the Dark Tower all tried
To be as was expected, not themselves.

[Sonnet 152]

We watch contrasting images of the corporate *apparatchik* sliding in and out the doors of his lunar megalometropolitan landscape and the honest English working man and bathos of the history of the British Labour Party.

The modern Roland's chic post-modern world of surgically hygienic, sterilised art museums is placed alongside a last snapshot of Vincent.

Childe Roland to the Dark Tower came and, having passed under the Tower of Auschwitz, penetrated deep into a void of art finance and corporate towers. We have come to the end of the modern world; we have come to the end of the poem of the same name:

Ask not what end, inquiring traveller,
Is served, what grim need to placate a god
Or worship him, what visions, definitions of
Our destiny, our purpose threw up these
Audacious towers to shine in evening light.
The sun, a crucible of nuclear rage,
Knows nothing of such ends: it thrummed out rays
Of heat until the ooze transformed itself.
Money's convulsions too are life-giving,
Neutral, imply no purpose in our hearts,
But blaze upon this rock to make Manhattan
Rise in resplendence, such a culmination
Of history seen at sunset from the harbour,
Meaningless, astonishing and simple.

[Sonnet 179]

Inevitably the outline I have presented is but a crude Cook's Tour through the poem. Better to consider again on the one hand the technique of the poem and on the other hand the grand themes of the book, which occur over and over, the great preoccupations and the ways they are so personally, immediately dealt with, yet with all the transfigurative grace that maybe only poetry can deliver.

There is the grand theme of the individual conscience in relation to society in history; the medieval warrior and his comitatus; the revolutionary leader and his chosen few; the avant-garde artist and his followers; man with woman and child; Childe Roland and his loyal band; the corporate magnate and his executives.

Most moving is Cronin's chronicle of modern English life. The poem is a direct response to the cry of William Blake:

I will not cease from mental fight
Nor shall my sword sleep in my hand
Till we have built Jerusalem
In England's green and pleasant land.

[*Milton*]

Apart from Mahon and the MacNeice of 'Autumn Journal' no other Irish poet has been so attuned to the English experience or has been able to write with such empathy about England, the English nation, and England's modern fate, not only on the large canvas of the civil war between Thatcher's Britain and Scargill's Britain but on the miniature household gods of domestic existence:

We went to Brighton in our Little Nine,
The open touring model Leslie bought
On what was called H.P. A gorgeous day,
The sky was somehow deep, you know, like heaven,
I thought the bubbling tar might melt the tyres
And Leslie laughed, called me a silly juggins.
He was a lovely driver, doing forty

Once we were free of Staines. It's tommy rot
To tell us now that people weren't happy.
We had our own nice house, a tudor villa,
Which was the new thing then, a vacuum cleaner,
Dance music on the wireless, lovely murders.
Of course the war was still to come, that Hitler,
But it all seemed somehow new then, somehow modern.

[Sonnet 95]

As well as a tear or two, those lines bring smiles to our faces. The comic note is achieved throughout the poem, the pure anarchic note which few poets ever achieve:

When Patrick Kavanagh's mother took him to
The circus which had come to Inniskeen,
They saw among the other acts a man
Lifting enormous weights and staggering
Bow-legged around the ring, his biceps, eyeballs,
Bulging with fearful effort. After that
He lay down on a bed of pointed nails.
Attendants placed a plank across his chest.
Ten bashful local louts were then invited
To stand across it, their combined weight being
About half a ton. The poet observed
It seemed a hard way for a man to earn
His living; but his mother said it was
Better than working anyway, she thought.

[Sonnet 159]

I see and hear Cronin as an evolution of Leopold Bloom; walker of the city; savourer of the minuscule and the vast. Aesthetically as well as ethically, one of the most satisfying triumphs of the poem is the fact that Cronin adopts no persona and yet he manages to distinguish subtly for the reader which 'he' is being referred to at any one point. One might say that the entire poem is about a certain 'he' and yet there is that 'he' there and this 'he' here. Not to mention the 'he' who is Anthony Cronin. There is a marvellous sleight of hand in Cronin's technique and the reader feels like a child breathless at the ringside of a circus of magicians.

When an artwork makes a guest appearance in verse it invariably appears as ornament or conceit or toy or mere object but in Cronin when paintings occur, they occur as vital organs of the anatomy of the poem. Reading Cronin's great Argenteuil sonnet (48) we know that Cronin has swallowed whole *The Luncheon of the Boating Party*, Renoir's greatest and most revolutionary painting and any one of Monet's many *La Grenouillère* paintings.

And yet although avant-garde art has always been a necessity to Cronin, there is nothing pictorial or descriptive in his own poetic technique. In Cronin's verse, the full-force gale of modern art has blown away all the visual clichés of Irish poetry.

Who else has written poetry about money? Cash, loot, tin, cabbage, lucre, moolah in detergent boxes? Infamously, Ezra Pound descanted about 'usury'. But, certainly alone among Irish poets, Cronin addresses the subject of money as we treat money in our everyday lives, perhaps the subject closest to our acquisitive, fatty little arteries, and the sorts of lies and delusions, greed and double-speak with which we girdle round this taboo topic. Another triumph of these sonnets.

In 1996 Cronin subtitled his biography of Samuel Beckett 'The Last Modernist'. In fact it is Cronin himself who is the seriously last modernist; a modernist who unlike Eliot, Pound and Beckett himself, has embraced modernity with all his soul, just as Hart Crane did in the 1920s. Throughout the poem there is the powerful current of Cronin's lyric passion for new engineering, new architecture, for wireless, cinema, airplanes and motor cars. Like Hart Crane, Cronin is the optimistic modernist, the lifelong born-again futurist. What Marinetti wrote in the first manifesto of Futurism in the *Figaro* in 1909 could just as easily have come from the lips of Cronin: 'a speeding automobile is more beautiful than the *Victory of Samothrace*.'

In the introduction to my commentary on *The End of the Modern World* I cited the *Canto*s of Ezra Pound and I did so with purposeful propriety. I stated that Cronin undertook the same project as Pound, to investigate the history of Western civilisation and to tell the story of the tribe, i.e. to write an *epic* poem. Many of Cronin's preoccupations are the same as Pound's and in his own idiom he achieves the same tone of easiness, Kavanagh's dead slack string. If I were requested to provide an epigraph for *The End of the Modern World* I would extract it from *The Pisan Cantos* of Ezra Pound:

> What thou lov'st well remains,
> > the rest is dross
> What thou lov'st well shall not be reft from thee
> What thou lov'st well is thy true heritage
> Whose world, or mine or theirs
> > or is it of none?
> First came the seen, then thus the palpable
> > Elysium, though it were in the halls of hell,
> What thou lovest well is thy true heritage
> What thou lov'st well shall not be reft from thee

In 1974 in a foreword to a Gallery Press edition of the *Selected Poems of James Clarence Mangan*, Anthony Cronin wrote apropos Mangan's poem 'The Nameless One': 'There is nothing rarer in poetry than a successful cry from the whole encircumscribed heart. This is one.' And so too is Cronin's own poem *The End of the Modern World*: a sensational achievement when you consider its length and scope. He is the direct lineal descendant of Oliver Goldsmith as he is of Johnson, Blake, Clough, Browning, Scott, Stevenson, Tennyson, and Housman, T. S. Eliot and Ezra Pound, W. H. Auden and Patrick Kavanagh. The recent winner of the T. S. Eliot Prize, George Szirtes, in an article in the *Irish Times* on 18 December 2004 concluded: 'Cronin is a major voice: he is Ireland's modern Dryden, a master of the public word in the public place.'

May it please the court, for your information: the text of *The End of the Modern World* is to be found in *Collected Poems*, Anthony Cronin, New Island Books, 2004, pp 159–258. I have made no reference to the greater corpus of Cronin's life's work in poetry which includes at least five or six other major poems of the twentieth century, notably *RMS Titanic*, first published in 1960 in the London literary review *X* (I:2); suffice to say that the œuvre is a treasure trove which will gleam from chasms in the rocks under the cliffs where once the city centre was, long after almost all of our contemporary volumes of verse have mouldered into unidentifiable dust.

I rest my case.

A transcript of a lecture given in Queen's University, Belfast, on 3 March 2005.

Hartnett's Farewell

The poet Michael Hartnett was born in west County Limerick in 1941 and died in Dublin in October 1999 aged fifty-eight. The myth of Hartnett is of an existentialist leprechaun, an enchanting but fanatical imbiber piping his way to an early grave. I recognise traces of the man in these images but they constitute a caricature that is far removed from the man I knew for almost forty years.

The myth of his poetry is of a collection almost exclusively of short poems. Again I acknowledge a shadowy veracity but again it is a misrepresentation. Hartnett was the author of longer poems beginning with his 'Tao' in 1963, and continuing with 'Anatomy of a Cliché' in 1968, 'The Hag of Beare' in 1969, 'A Farewell to English' in 1975, 'The Retreat of Ita Cagney' in 1975, 'Cúlú Ide' in 1975, 'Maiden Street Ballad' in 1980, 'An Phurgóid' in 1982, 'An Lia Nocht' in 1985, 'Inchicore Haiku' in 1985, 'Mountains, Fall on Us' in 1992, and culminating in 1994 in three of the most outstanding longer poems by any poet in Irish literature, first *The Man Who Wrote Yeats, the Man Who Wrote Mozart*, secondly *Sibelius in Silence* and, thirdly, *He'll to the Moors*. In these three longer poems I recognise the sophisticated, iconoclastic, analytical, encyclopaedic, cosmopolitan, droll, ironic, tragicomic poet I encountered in 1962. It is this Hartnett I want to consider and not the doomed hobgoblin of literary gossip. The Michael Hartnett I met in the early 1960s is well depicted by the words that the Finnish Swedish-language author Adolf Paul (1863–1942) used in his novel *A Book about a Man* (1891), to describe the young Sibelius in Berlin in the 1880s: 'He was a real natural genius, thoroughly individual. Without the slightest relationship to others.'

With my title 'Hartnett's Farewell' I am invoking 'Ó Riada's Farewell' which was the title given to the last recording of the composer Seán Ó Riada (1931–71) released posthumously by Claddagh Records in 1972. Ó Riada was a kindred spirit of Hartnett's in his confrontation with the Irish language and the Gaelic inheritance. The two men, however, never met and Ó Riada was dead by the time Hartnett made his drastic decision in 1975 to relocate from Dublin to West Limerick just as Ó Riada initiated a comparably drastic relocation from Dublin to West Cork in 1963. It is improbable that Hartnett did not have Ó Riada's example in mind.

Of these three longer poems, it is on *Sibelius in Silence* that I want to concentrate. It is the single most engrossing, most suggestive and most beautifully crafted poem that Michael Hartnett ever wrote and yet, since its first publication twelve years ago, I have encountered only one person who has read it, the poet Harry Clifton.

Sibelius in Silence, a poem of 195 lines, was inspired by Hartnett's lifelong preoccupation with the music and person of the Finnish composer Jean Sibelius (1865–1957). I recall Michael in 1962 in Dublin enthusing about Sibelius, especially about the orchestral work known as 'Finlandia', which was first performed in November 1899 as a protest against the tyranny of the Russian Tsar Nicholas II and which was and, I think, remains Finland's unofficial national anthem. Sibelius's 'Finlandia' is to Finns what O Riada's *Mise Éire* used to be to many Irish people or Elgar's 'Pomp and Circumstance' to the British.

As a result of Michael's enthusiasm, I purchased an LP of 'Finlandia', one of the first LPs I ever purchased and the first LP I purchased of what was termed 'serious' or 'classical' music. Michael used to hum and whistle snatches of 'Finlandia'. It was as if Michael was playing the part of the speaker in Thomas Kinsella's poem, 'I wonder whether one expects / Flowing tie or expert sex', which was published in the year of Michael's arrival in Dublin, 1962, in Kinsella's new volume, *Downstream*, a collection of poems admired by Michael:

I pat my wallet pocket, thinking
I can spare an evening drinking;

Humming as I catch the bus
Something by Sibelius

['Downstream']

But Michael was not playing any part; he was being himself, a lover of music of all kinds ranging from Elvis Presley and Buddy Holly to Irish traditional music to Mozart, Tchaikovsky, Schumann and, above all, Sibelius.

It was fitting, therefore, that thirty years later, in 1992 after a lifetime of writing his own kind of music – a verbal music known as poetry – that Hartnett should attempt a kind of *summa theologica* in the form of assuming the voice of Sibelius. (*Summa theologica* is an apt analogy because Hartnett was a student of Thomas Aquinas, the Angelic Doctor. Hartnett was himself a logician and, indeed, a theo-logician, a theologian, as he demonstrated in his poem *He'll to the Moors*.) In *Sibelius in Silence*, Sibelius is speaking in the voice of Michael Hartnett. A process of triple-take is at work in the poem.

Nearing the end of his life, Sibelius (in the voice of Hartnett) reflects on that life and on how it ended in thirty years of silence. In 1926 Sibelius published his symphonic tone poem 'Tapiola' and never published any music again until his death thirty-one years later in 1957. The poet Hartnett after the publication of *Sibelius in Silence* in 1994 was to write no more serious original poetry. He died in 1999.

In Hartnett's poem Sibelius reflects also on the history and prehistory of Finland and on his own dilemma of having being born a Swedish-speaking Finn in a Finland tyrannised by Tsarist Russia, who did not begin to learn and speak Finnish until the age of eight. In the poem we hear Sibelius brooding on the perennial conundrums of race, language and landscape; of the relationship of aboriginal peoples to later waves of immigration; of the tension between original inhabitants and planters. Hartnett has Sibelius laconically observe: 'for even planters tend to meditation'.

All of these questions are the questions which dominated Hartnett's own life and which first found large expression in his infamous 'A Farewell to English', in 1975. I say 'infamous' for two reasons:

first, it was misrepresented by the various cultural, academic, media and political factions in the Ireland of the 1970s; and, secondly, it is not in the top flight of Hartnett's poetry in the sense that *Sibelius in Silence* is.

Two-thirds of the way into the poem Hartnett takes up the theme of alcohol, a subject which was at the centre of the lives and works of both Sibelius and Hartnett. The climax of the poem represents Sibelius conducting his own *Fourth Symphony* which of all Sibelius's works is the most crucial. The poem concludes with Sibelius's vehement, wise, Lear-like meditation on his thirty years of silence.

Sibelius in Silence
for Angela Liston

To have intricacies of lakes and forests,
harbours, hills, and inlets given –
and none of these with a name;
then to have posited nomads straggling
from the barricading Urals
bearing on their backs and horses
children, language, and utensils,
gods and legends;
then to have brought all these together,
yeast to the thawing mud –
this was to make in the Green Gold of the North
an ethnic and enduring bread.

They settled where their dead
were buried and gave names
to every hill and harbour,
names that might become unspoken
but would forever whisper 'Not yours'
to mapping strangers;
their dead became the land they lived on,
became the very lakes and corries,

the very myths and shadows that live
inside the birch and pine tree;
their dead sprung up in grains and berries
nourishing their offspring
that inhabited the cold expanses.
They sowed their gods in caves and hillsides,
gods that might become forgotten
but would forever whisper 'Go home'
to dreaming strangers.

After the land is first immersed
in language, gods, and legends,
sown with blood and bodies,
whatever strangers come and conquer
and stand upon the hills at evening
(for even planters tend to meditation)
they will sense they are not wanted here;
for the wind, the old, old voices
moulding ice and snowdrifts
into Arctic intimations of the shapes,
now quite unhuman, they possess
in a dead and parallel present,
will tell them:
'You are not ours, you are not wanted,'
and the lake, the pine, the birch tree,
the very slope and curve of mountain,
all will say the same:
'The name you call us by is not our name.'

Whoever comes and conquers –
from the first flake of fish eaten,
from the first crumb of bread taken
in this place –
blood in water and in ground

transubstantiates that race
and performs an altering justice;
its homeland becomes myth;
its very customs, clothing, accent
(if not language) change
and now are woven
from other soils and other souls
in this intricate biosphere.
It is not wanted here
nor loved at home;
it watches rivers wash
its labels from their banks
contemptuously to sea,
watches names it put on hills
detach themselves and doggedly slide down
a valley of unwanted nouns.
It sits inside its palisade
and sees its gods move out of reach
and fade
before the bright gods of the older race,
its children's mouths ringed purple
with their speech.
When I was young I did not know their language.
I visited the inns of Babel
where old and young drank mugs of syntax
that turned on tongues and hands to music,
where men at beer-ringed counters
told me their melodious open secrets
and I held up identity papers
and said, 'I *do* belong: this *is* my country',
and they let me join their ranks –
for part of me indeed throughout the centuries
had become this race's;
and although my origins still slunk

some thousand years away
in heavily guarded strong-rooms in my head
their edges had the tint,
had absorbed the purple hue
that revealed I ate
the berries that the conquered grew;
all this (papers, costume, customs,
fibre transformed and muscles
and my longing to belong)
was negated by my voice,
my traitor larynx
that then could never frame
their simplest proverb
or sing their simplest song –
but courtesy is not acceptance
so I left the friendly inns
and walked into the dark,
landmarks all around me
hinting at the road,
and a calvary of signposts
on which strange names were shown
that pointed out the way
but not the way home.

Blacker than the blackest swans are,
all my life their mythic figures
clothed in insistent rhythms
have pursued me and made me anxious,
called my name, and demanded answers:
and I listened. And I answered.
Music was my language, so I gave them my music;
and the land drank in my music.
Caught at school in webs of grammar
which still at night enmesh my face,

I had no tongue in the land I came from
but at first, at best, a stammer;
but the fluency I sought I found
in the speech that underlies my music.
The land took me in her embrace;
I wed the land and dreamed her freedom
somehow coalesced and marched *maestoso*
out through the hatchings of my music-sheets.
But the people heard the real programme:
the *crescendi* of shells in the air
and their climax in the streets.

'Alcohol's a cunning beast.
It fools the doctor and the priest,
it fools the clever and the sane –
but not the liver or the brain.'
Idle verses, so I thought
that someone, doodling, idly makes.
But now blood breaks like snowflakes
from my brothers' nostrils
and my hand shakes.
I gave everything I could:
music, speeches, pat harangues;
intellectualised the fight
and, *tremblando*, wept *adagios*, wrung my hands –
in short, spilled every drink but blood.
Autumn breaks its rainbows
along the staggering trees
and my hand quivers.
Into my room across my music-sheets
sail black swans on blacker rivers.

They say my music weeps for the days
when my people ate the bark from trees

because all crops had failed.
Music disdains such theories:
I offer you here cold, pure water –
as against the ten-course tone-poems,
the indigestible Mahlerian feasts;
as against the cocktails' many hues,
all liquors crammed in one glass –
pure, cold water is what I offer.
Composed, I am conducting. It is my
fourth symphony, third movement and,
as my baton tries to make the music keep
to the key of C sharp minor,
vodka ebbs in tremors from my hand
and at the ragged corner of my eye
a raven flies through the concert hall
and I find a self saying to myself,
'It was the deer that stripped the trees,
 not the people at all.'
Two flutes grapple with an ice-cold note
until the 'cello takes command.
As the audience's hiss escapes
splinters of birch-bark stick in my throat.

And now, because I made such strict demands
upon my art, I must dismiss such music as intrudes
on me as I conceal my shaking hands.
No loss indeed – it's now quite trivial and crude;
no more legends come out of the northern lands,
no more Virgins of the Air, no more black swans,
no more seamless symphonies project themselves.
I take down a book of poetry from my shelves
to share with my children's children the old store
of verses that this green-gold land reveres
(I speak their native language fluently

but when excited lapse into my planters' tongue).
You may think thirty years of silence far too long
but some composers now about should have learnt from me
that silence would have graced the world far more
than their gutting and dismembering of song.
And that which was part of me has not left me yet –
however etherialised, I still know when it's there.
I get up at odd hours of the night
or snap from a doze deep in a chair;
I shuffle to the radio, switch on the set,
and pluck, as I did before, *Finlandia* out of the air.

In his title *Sibelius in Silence* Hartnett is saying, I think, that the art of poetry is about concentration striving to become contemplation.

The eloquence and yet the simplicity of the introductory three verse paragraphs are among the most beautiful lines Hartnett ever wrote. To my ear they equal what T. S. Eliot in the same vein attempted in *Four Quartets*. (Eliot was the first and greatest English-language influence in Hartnett's writing life, followed by Ezra Pound, with, in the background, William Yeats.)

The viewpoint of the opening lines is godlike. The tone of voice, together with its statement, is of God holding out the globe of the world in the palm of his hand and considering the galactic orb as if it were a mathematical theorem or a puzzle for a chess master; and, indeed, Hartnett was an excellent practitioner of chess and he had that kind of abstract, logical cast of mind that Sibelius also had.

To have intricacies of lakes and forests,
harbours, hills, and inlets given –
and none of these with a name;
then to have posited nomads straggling
from the barricading Urals
bearing on their backs and horses
children, language, and utensils,

gods and legends;
then to have brought all these together,
yeast to the thawing mud –
this was to make in the Green Gold of the North
an ethnic and enduring bread.

But while the angle is godlike and the voice is Sibelius, the vocabulary is Hartnettian: words and phrases such as 'intricacies', 'posited', 'yeast', 'ethnic and enduring bread', 'nomads straggling' and 'the barricading Urals' are peculiar to Hartnett.

Writing with the authority of the master poet, Hartnett is able to introduce one of his central themes as early as the third line: 'and none of these with a name'. For Hartnett, the key to human existence is the strange music of human language and the strange human need to name places. Heidegger liked to invoke Hölderlin's sentence 'Linguistically man dwelleth on earth.' In the third line Hartnett is reiterating that basic insight of Hölderlin's and Heidegger's. (In the early 1960s, Hartnett read as much of Heidegger as he could find in English translation.)

Note also the phrase in the fourth line 'nomads straggling'. Hartnett does not speak of, say, 'Mesolithic hunter-gatherers migrating', an illustration of the difference between the art of poetry and the scientific discipline of archaeology. The poet Hartnett, striving for as linguistically profound a precision as is poetically possible, is saying that man in his origins was a nomad who straggled, not a typology that migrated.

In the second paragraph Hartnett presents cemeteries as the first settlements of Finland. Simultaneously he is depicting also the prehistory of Ireland. (One of Hartnett's own personal holy places was the prehistoric settlement of Lough Gur in County Limerick, twenty-five miles north north-east of Hartnett's hometown of Newcastle West.)

Hartnett establishes an absolute anthropological datum, which is that a human being's first language is the language of place names. For Hartnett, the tradition of the *dindsenchas* is not only a practice in Gaelic poetry but a universal human norm. Hartnett in his person and poetry was the embodiment of Estyn Evans's pronouncement that 'geography is ultimately more important than genes'. Born into an English-speaking small-town working-class family in County Limerick in 1941 Hartnett heard the ancient landscape of Ireland, Éire, Banbha, Fodhla speak to him across intervals of thousands of years and the language of the landscape might have been Gaelic but possibly might have predated Gaelic, some remote, unknown species of Indo-European. Sibelius, born into a Swedish-speaking district of Finland in 1865, heard the ancient Finnish words and perhaps even older words.

Depicting how human settlement grows out of burial grounds, Hartnett delves into a metaphor of the Eucharistic character of death – how the living eat the dead:

> their dead sprung up in grains and berries
> nourishing their offspring

Since the Second World War we have become accustomed to commentators such as Edward Said or Terry Eagleton analysing the dominant role of the coloniser in the relationship between colonialism and native populations. In the fourth paragraph of the poem Hartnett takes up this theme but holds up for our inspection a reverse process in which he perceives the native population as the dominant partner in the relationship. Hartnett depicts how 'blood and water' of the indigenous dead 'transubstantiates' the coloniser and, in a felicitous phrase, 'performs an altering justice'. (Note the ease with which Hartnett can introduce a technical theological term such as 'transubstantiates'; it is necessary to remember always that although he was not a conventional church-goer, Hartnett was steeped in Christian theology, liturgy and mysticism; not only was it, spiritually speaking, his mother tongue but it was also one of his abiding intellectual preoccupations as illustrated most dramatically in the third of the three major longer poems of his farewell period – *He'll to the Moors* – and also in his translations into Gaelic Irish of the poetry of St John of the Cross.)

Hartnett, the master of the extended metaphor, proceeds to depict the body physic of the landscape of Finland rejecting the serum of the invading languages of Swedish and Russian. When I read this passage,

[40]

I am reminded of the play *Translations* and Brian Friel's English carto-
graphers in all their ignorant naivety mapping and re-naming in
English the Gaelic landscape of County Donegal:

It is not wanted here
nor loved at home;
it watches rivers wash
its labels from their banks
contemptuously to sea,
watches names it put on hills
detach themselves and doggedly slide down
a valley of unwanted nouns.
It sits inside its palisade
and sees its gods move out of reach
and fade
before the bright gods of the older race,
its children's mouths ringed purple
with their speech.

From the landscape of Finland Hartnett transports the Sibelian
voice to the hinterland of his native town of Newcastle West in County
Limerick and his childhood and young manhood in and around the public
houses of remote and exotic and obscure locations such as Strand and
Killeedy and Camas. We see the young Hartnett of the 1940s and the
1950s at the feet of his Gaelic-speaking grandmother and her cronies
and other anonymous elders of the tribe who lurk in dark corners like
presences out of a Jack B. Yeats painting. These are the borderlands of
Slieve Luachra, the world of Padraig O'Keeffe, the fabled fiddler. The
boy Hartnett, born into a small-town working-class English-speaking
family, longs to belong to the ancient, rural, Gaelic-speaking, aristo-
cratic tribe but again and again he is betrayed and embarrassed by
what he terms his 'traitor larynx':

When I was young I did not know their language.
I visited the inns of Babel
where old and young drank mugs of syntax

that turned on tongues and hands to music,
where men at beer-ringed counters
told me their melodious open secrets
and I held up identity papers
and said, 'I *do* belong; this *is* my country',
and they let me join their ranks –
for part of me indeed throughout the centuries
had become this race's

Following on that typical Hartnett play on conventional imagery – his 'inns of Babel' instead of 'towers of Babel' – there occurs a water-marked Hartnettian aphorism that had been recurring in his verse since its beginnings in the late 1950s: 'but courtesy is not acceptance'. No matter how many hours and years he spends in the inns of Babel and Strand and Newcastle West he remains outcast:

so I left the friendly inns
and walked into the dark,
landmarks all around me
hinting at the road,
and a calvary of signposts
on which strange names were shown
that pointed out the way
but not the way home.

A shocking, yet simple image – 'a calvary of signposts'.

The signposts of rural Ireland in the last half century have been ten-foot poles with beak-shaped white plates bearing black characters of place names. Hartnett is preparing us for the black swans that intro-duce his next paragraph, the black swans that haunted Sibelius's life and work:

Blacker than the blackest swans are
all my life their mythic figures
clothed in insistent rhythms

have pursued me and made me anxious,
called my name, and demanded answers:
and I listened. And I answered.

Hartnett's line 'Blacker than the blackest swans are' is an almost direct
transcription from an entry for 22 November 1917 in Sibelius's diary as
quoted by Erik Tawaststjerna in volume three of Tawaststjerna's defin-
itive biography of Sibelius: 'Saw a swan today. It was rocked by the
waves at the edge of the ice ... There are moments in life when every-
thing is blacker than black – darker than night.' Since his youth and his
discovery of the legends of the Finnish national epic the *Kalevala* (the
Kalevala or 'Land of Heroes' was compiled and published by Elias
Lonnrot in 1849 as part of the pan-European rediscovery of national
folklore and it played the same role in the evolution of Finnish political
independence as the Cuchulain cycle along with the Children of Lir
and other myths played in Irish history), Sibelius had been obsessed by
the legend of the black swans of Tuonela in Rune XIV of the *Kalevala*
and as early as 1893 he wrote one of his most celebrated compositions,
the tone poem entitled 'The Swan of Tuonela'. Tuonela is the kingdom
of death and around its perimeter circles the fast-flowing black waters
of the river of Tuonela on which rides eternally the Black Swan of the
Kingdom of Death. The hero Lemminkäinen sets out to shoot dead
with a crossbow the black swan as a gift for his bride but instead is shot
dead himself by a herdsman of Pohjola.

Music was my language, so I gave them my music;

To conform to the iambic pentameter line most poets would have
omitted the second possessive adjective 'my' but Hartnett has the
nerve to go for the grace note and so, against the rules, he inserts the
second possessive adjective 'my' so you get 'Music was my language, so
I gave them my music'.

Hartnett's dramaturgy is analogous to the invention at the heart of
Friel's *Translations*. Just as in *Translations* we are confronted by actors
playing nineteenth-century Donegal peasants who are speaking Gaelic

in English, so in Hartnett's poem he contrives to convince us that his language is music through the medium of the language of poetry; more subtly, we know that Hartnett's language is poetry and yet by his doubling as Sibelius, he is able to convince us that his language is music. Locking us into this double double-take, Hartnett then goes for broke with a triple-take by reverting in the next line to the auto-biographical conceit of linguistic communication being his first language:

> Caught at school in webs of grammar
> which still at night enmesh my face,
> I had no tongue in the land I came from
> but at first, at best, a stammer

Pirouetting on the tightrope of his high wire act, Hartnett drags us up to yet another level – to the domain of the *dindsenchas*, a feature of Gaelic Irish poetry comparable to the topographical poetry of the *Kalevala* – and in so doing opens up us readers into the realms of *Mise Éire* and 'Finlandia':

> The land took me in her embrace;
> I wed the land and dreamed her freedom
> somehow coalesced and marched *maestoso*
> out through the hatchings of my music-sheets.
> But the people heard the real programme:
> the *crescendi* of shells in the air
> and their climax in the streets.

Simultaneously, we are in Dublin in 1916 outside the GPO, and in Helsinki in 1917 as the October revolution in Russia prefigures civil war and revolution in Finland.

In the next paragraph or movement of Hartnett's poem – I say 'movement' because there is an obvious orchestral structure to the poem – Hartnett switches key and hammers out two heroic couplets to introduce the theme of the role of alcohol in the Finnish composer's life as well as in his own life:

> *'Alcohol's a cunning beast.*
> *It fools the doctor and the priest,*
> *it fools the clever and the sane –*
> *but not the liver or the brain.'*

Whereupon, Hartnett drops the heroic couplet as abruptly as he initiated it and slows down to a free verse alternating rhymes with non-rhymes and short lines with longer lines as he paints a portrait of the terrifying black sobriety of the composer who made a quasi-Faustian pact with alcohol; Hartnett's metrical picture-making of a nosebleed as a snowstorm, and of forests falling down, and of the trembling of hands culminates in an apotheosis of black swans, the victory of death over life:

> Idle verses, so I thought
> that someone, doodling, idly makes.
> But now blood breaks like snowflakes
> from my brothers' nostrils
> and my hand shakes.
> I gave everything I could:
> music, speeches, pat harangues;
> intellectualised the fight
> and, *tremblando*, wept *adagios*, wrung my hands –
> in short, spilled every drink but blood.
> Autumn breaks its rainbows
> along the staggering trees
> and my hand quivers.
> Into my room across my music-sheets
> sail black swans on blacker rivers.

Alcohol was as essential a concomitant of Sibelius's life and work as it was of Hartnett's life and work from 1980 to his death nineteen years later in 1999. Here is an entry from Sibelius's diary for 16 September 1916 when he was fifty-one years old, the same age as was Michael Hartnett when he wrote *Sibelius in Silence*:

> Went into town yesterday and the day before. Heavy drinking and afterwards much depression. Terrible this state. Particularly as my weakness for alcohol damages me in my own and others' eyes. At home here some furtive drinking to get my nerves in better condition. (quoted in Tawaststjerna, *Sibelius*, vol. 3)

Sibelius's biographer Erik Tawaststjerna records that in the following year of 1917 Sibelius's handwriting was affected by alcohol: 'His writing becomes rounder and broader, as are the diary entries themselves – repetitions, rhetorical questions and exclamation marks.'

In a diary entry in April 1919 Sibelius is alarmed by the tremor in his hands:

> It would be an easy thing for me to work if cheap and weak wines were ready to hand. These days I am drinking whisky and schnapps. My hands shake so much that I can't write. (vol. 3)

His biographer comments: 'One wonders whether he in fact needed a regular intake of alcohol to steady his tremor! After his long period of temperance from 1908 to 1915 and further enforced abstinence during 1918, his drinking and tremor became something of a vicious circle; the drinking produced a tremor, which could then be stabilised only by further drink.'

In a diary entry for 11 February 1920 Sibelius writes:

> Scored *Valse Lyrique*. This orchestration has entailed enormous work, so much so that my hands tremble and I can't work at it without stopping from time to time. Only wine seems to steady me – and at present prices! (vol. 3)

Two weeks later he writes:

> My hands no longer tremble. It feels strange to be able to write normally. (vol. 3)

Towards the end of the year on 27 November 1920 he notes:

> Am curing myself with whisky and have already made considerable progress. (vol. 3)

Five days later on 2 December 1920 he adds:

> Cheer up – death is around the corner. (vol. 3)

Three years later on 11 November 1923 he writes:

> Alcohol, which I gave up, is now my most faithful companion. And the most understanding! Everything and everyone else have largely failed me. (vol. 3)

In the following year, he writes:

> At nights I compose. No, at nights I sit at my desk with a bottle of whisky and try to work. Later, I wake, my head upon the score and my hand clasped round empty air. Aino [his wife] has removed the whisky while I sleep. (vol. 3)

Four years further along the road, on 8 May 1927 he writes:

> In order to survive, I have to have alcohol. Wine or whisky. (vol. 3)

Any or all of those diary entries by Sibelius could have been penned by Michael Hartnett in his own diary for the years 1980 to 1999. It is necessary for the understanding of Hartnett's poem *Sibelius in Silence* as well as for an understanding of his entire œuvre that we clarify Hartnett's view of the role of alcohol in art and life, for he had a definite and even more logical view of alcohol than Sibelius did.

In the early 1960s in Dublin Michael Hartnett spent a great deal of time in the pubs but he was different from all the other drinkers in that he was contemptuous of the culture of alcohol that ruled at that time, especially in the literary pubs. I remember being shocked in 1962 by the severity of his strictures. He acknowledged the ruthlessness of his attitude and warned me that it was morally necessary for his and my survival.

There were three types of drinker whom he condemned: firstly, the elder writer publicly in the grip of alcohol addiction. Hartnett felt that no poet worthy of the name should allow himself to become vulnerable to such an extent. Secondly, Bohemian drinkers who regarded it as obligatory to offer up one's life on the altar of alcohol, and who preached a cult of alcohol. Thirdly, the lawyer-journalist-academic types who were so besotted with alcohol that no matter how witty their conversations and writings, their thinking was sodden with booze.

I was shocked because Hartnett's attitudes were so non-conformist. To take this stance in the early 1960s was to be a heretic and to stand outside everybody. I admired his independence of mind and the courage it required. He struck me as a kind of mid twentieth-century reincarnation of the young James Joyce. His ruthless common sense could be mistaken for arrogance and his high standards for conceit. Hartnett knew his own mind as only the real poet does know it.

I say 'real' poet. I have met many writers of verse in my life but very few poets. Hartnett was a poet – a real poet. For him the writing of poetry was a vocation, an all-or-nothing calling.

Twenty years later in 1983 Hartnett's marriage, under attack from economic attrition and his own intellectual isolation, began to break up and with it his family home and life in the hills of Templeglantine in West Limerick. The end when it came, came suddenly and overnight at the end of 1984 he found himself alone, marooned and homeless in Dublin. I believe that being the ruthlessly logical artist that he was, he calculated that in order to survive as a poet in Dublin city he would be compelled to drink hard liquor in extreme and regular quantities. I believe he made a secret pact with himself in the privacy of his own soul. Knowing full well that the price would be an early death but believing that it was the only method of living whereby he would be able to continue writing poetry, Michael Hartnett dedicated the rest of his life to a black sobriety of a kind very similar to, only more extreme than that employed by Sibelius.

Hartnett and Sibelius were similar personalities. Robert Layton writes that Sibelius was a cordial *bon viveur* and connoisseur of food, drink and tobacco, constantly in financial difficulties, small in stature, who suffered from melancholia and yet was wonderful fun: 'spontaneous, warm, and immediate ... impulsive, instinctive, generous'. All of which is a precise evocation of the personality of Hartnett.

Having stated starkly the theme of alcohol Hartnett proceeds to the climax of the poem: a meditation by Sibelius as he beholds himself both composing and conducting his *Fourth Symphony*, the darkest, the most radical and most beautiful of all his works, known sometimes as the *Barkbrod* (the bark bread) *Symphony* because Sibelius had in mind famine times in the nineteenth century, when Finns used to grind birch tree bark and mix it with flour to make bread. The voices of Hartnett and Sibelius are interchangeable as he remarks at the beginning of the seventh paragraph:

> They say my music weeps for the days
> when my people ate the bark from trees
> because all crops had failed.
> Music disdains such theories:
> I offer you here cold, pure water –
> as against the ten-course tone-poems,
> the indigestible Mahlerian feasts;
> as against the cocktails' many hues,
> all liquors crammed in one glass –
> pure, cold water is what I offer.

Hartnett here is quoting from the composer's diary in which Sibelius recalls a visit to Germany:

> In Germany, they took me to hear some new music. I said, 'You are manufacturing cocktails of all colours. And here I come with pure cold water.' My music is molten ice. In its movement you may detect its frozen beginnings, in its sonorities you may detect its initial silence.

Panning across the œuvre of Sibelius, Hartnett zooms in on the notes that begin the third movement of the *Fourth Symphony*: two solo flutes playing so mutely, hesitantly as if not really playing but tentatively tuning up, frozen fingers struggling to warm up in a polar landscape against the rising winds of double-bass and cello, basset-horn and bassoon, viola and violins and brass. The *Fourth Symphony* but in particular the third movement epitomises that epigrammatic concentration in form and content that both Sibelius and Hartnett always strove after. Throughout this great verse paragraph Hartnett has in mind the historic conversation in Helsinki in 1907 between Sibelius and Mahler, which Sibelius wrote up in his diary:

> When our conversation touched upon the symphony, I said that I admired its style and severity of form and the profound logic that created an inner connection between all the motifs ... (quoted in Tawaststjerna, *Sibelius*, vol. 2)

Mahler protested against Sibelius's austerity. 'No, no,' cried Mahler, 'the symphony must be like the world – it must contain everything.'
In the middle of this verse paragraph, Hartnett's verse line achieves what Kavanagh called 'the sonorous beat':

> Composed, I am conducting. It is my
> fourth symphony, third movement and,
> as my baton tries to make the music keep

to the key of C sharp minor,
vodka ebbs in tremors from my hand
and at the ragged corner of my eye
a raven flies through the concert hall
and I find a self saying to myself,
'It was the deer that stripped the trees,
not the people at all.'
Two flutes grapple with an ice-cold note
until the 'cello takes command.
As the audience's hiss escapes
splinters of birch-bark stick in my throat.

Hartnett's phrase 'the audience's hiss' illustrates how steeped he was in the primary sources of Sibelius's life. In the many books by Sibelius's foremost English-language chronicler, Robert Layton, it is the word 'hiss' that is used to describe the audience's reaction to the January 1913 performance of the *Fourth Symphony* in Gothenburg.

The raven that flies through the concert hall is the raven of Edgar Allen Poe's poem *The Raven*, with which Sibelius was obsessed during the writing of the finale of the fourth movement of the *Fourth Symphony*, and in which the American gothic poet is sitting up alone in the small hours exactly as Michael Hartnett used do in his second-storey flat at 23 Upper Leeson Street and, as he portrays Sibelius in the poem, dozing in his armchair. The poet asks the raven if he will ever meet again his dead love Lenore: 'Quoth the Raven, "Nevermore."' The Raven of Poe's poem is that eternal oblivion of which each and every human being lives in dread:

'Be that word our sign of parting, bird or fiend!' I
    shrieked, upstarting –
'Get thee back into the tempest and the Night's
    Plutonian shore!
Leave no black plume as a token of that lie thy soul
    hath spoken!

Leave my loneliness unbroken! – quit the bust above
    my door!
Take thy beak from out my heart, and take thy form
    from off my door!'
                    Quoth the Raven, 'Nevermore.'

In 1908 Sibelius had been diagnosed with cancer of the throat and believed with good reason that he was facing certain death. Hartnett with his Sibelian-like technique of economy in verse underscores all of this with a confrontation with mythology: did the Finns of former times have recourse to eating the bark from birch trees? Or was it the deer who stripped the birches? By implication Hartnett is also questioning our own Irish mythologies of self-pity and self-delusion. But Hartnett, I think, is also hinting that it is he and Sibelius who ate the bark from trees. In the solitude and desolation of their art they were reduced to eating bark from trees; that was the price each paid.

But the ultimate price was silence and death. In the end, Hartnett's poem is about his conviction that the end of art is silence; that, as in Anthony Cronin's words apropos Beckett, 'the object of true, achieved and necessary utterance is silence' (*The Last Modernist*, p. 376). Sibelius had written in his diary:

What happens when music ceases? Silence. All the other arts aspire to the condition of music. What does music aspire to? Silence.

In the eighth and final paragraph or movement of the poem, Hartnett announces Sibelius's renunciation of his art:

And now, because I made such strict demands
upon my art, I must dismiss such music as intrudes
on me as I conceal my shaking hands.
No loss indeed – it's now quite trivial and crude;

What poet other than Hartnett would have such severe and stoic honesty to dismiss his own last verses as 'quite trivial and crude'?

[52]

His brother-in-arms, Mahon, perhaps.

In a final chess-mate of triple-take metamorphosis, the poet Hartnett has the composer Sibelius take down from his shelves a book of the poetry of the *Kalevala* so that he can pass on these poems, not his music, to his grandchildren:

> I take down a book of poetry from my shelves
> to share with my children's children the old store
> of verses that this green-gold land reveres
> (I speak their native language fluently
> but when excited lapse into my planters' tongue).

Once again I marvel at Hartnett's book-learning when in Robert Layton's volume entitled *Sibelius* in a footnote on p. 64 I read: 'According to Mrs Lauri Kirves, the composer's grand-daughter, Sibelius mostly spoke Finnish with the grandchildren, though in moments of excitement he would revert to Swedish.' (And I am even more astonished when I learn from Michael's partner Angela Liston that although Michael did own a copy of this particular volume by Layton, it was the 1978 edition, not the 1992 revised edition.)

Sibelius/Hartnett reproaches his younger contemporaries for the lack of substance in their verse:

> You may think thirty years of silence far too long
> but some composers now about should have learnt from me
> that silence would have graced the world far more
> than their gutting and dismembering of song.

Michael Hartnett rejected the mass production of superfluous verse; the poet's obligation, as he understood it, was to produce only utterance of necessity.

Hartnett's own theory of poetic practice was kindred to Sibelius's theory of musical composition. In his diary entry for 1 August 1912 Sibelius wrote:

I let the musical thought and its development in my mind determine matters of form. I'd compare a symphony to a river: the river is made up of countless streams all looking for an outlet: the innumerable tributaries, streams and brooks that form the river before it broadens majestically and flows into the sea. The movement of the water determines the shape of the river bed: the movement of the river water is the flow of the musical ideas and the river bed that they form is the symphonic structure. (quoted in Layton, *Sibelius*, p. 5)

Sibelius in music like Hartnett in poetry had an avant-garde belief in the river-deep connection between improvisation and organic form.

The poem draws *diminuendo* to its close as in a late Friel play:

And that which was part of me has not left me yet –
however etherialised, I still know when it's there.
I get up at odd hours of the night
or snap from a doze deep in a chair;
I shuffle to the radio, switch on the set,
and pluck, as I did before, *Finlandia* out of the air.

Thus concludes one of the major poems in the Irish landscape of the last two hundred years. The tone of voice is pure Hartnettian and the vivid image is of the poet himself in the living room of his flat at 23 Upper Leeson Street half-asleep in the mid-hours of night, abruptly waking up and climbing to his feet, shuffling across the room and, as he says, plucking 'Finlandia' – or 'The Retreat of Ita Cagney' – from the air. Robert Layton's last words on the *Fourth Symphony* apply also to Hartnett's poem: 'There is a searching intensity here, a purity of utterance, and a vision and insight of rare quality' (Layton, *Sibelius*, p. 82).

It is exhilarating to observe also that even here at the closing of the poem Hartnett perseveres in sticking to the primary sources of Sibelius's life. These last lines are almost a direct transcription from a statement of Sibelius's wife Aino (quoted in David Burnett-James's book on Sibelius published in 1989 when Hartnett was composing his poem):

He was thought by his closest associates to be psychic – 'not dependent only on five senses', as his secretary put it. His wife believed he was aware when one of his works was being broadcast anywhere in the world. 'He is sitting quietly reading a book or newspaper. Suddenly he becomes restless, goes to the radio, turns the knobs, and then one of his symphonies or tone-poems comes out of the air.' (p. 99)

But what about Hartnett's aside that precedes the final scene of the dozing composer?

And that which was part of me has not left me yet –
however etherialised, I still know when it's there.

What is still there? What is that part of Hartnett which has not left him yet? First, it is his faith in his calling as a poet and in the art of poetry. 'He was grounded in poetry. It kept his feet on the earth', wrote Anthony Cronin in the *Sunday Independent* four days after Hartnett's death. Secondly, it is his humanity, and that defiant belief that Hartnett had in man's common humanity and in its childlike essence. Over a lifetime's dedication to his art, Hartnett reiterated his credo in human and humane values and his repudiation of all the perversions of language, most especially the language of propaganda, euphemism and cliché. He understood his vocation in exactly the same terms as did Eliot and Mallarmé, 'to purify the dialect of the tribe'.

Yet *Sibelius in Silence* remains a tragic poem. Michael Hartnett had a 'tragic sense of life', to borrow the words of the title of one of the books that he cherished in his youth in the early 1960s, the Spanish classic wisdom-book *The Tragic Sense of Life* by Miguel de Unamuno.

Sibelius in Silence, along with its companion poems, *The Man Who Wrote Yeats, the Man Who Wrote Mozart*, and *He'll to the Moors* constitutes the last poetry of Michael Hartnett. Apart from a few of what he termed 'strays' and his translations from the seventeenth- and eighteenth-century Gaelic Irish poetry of Haicéad and Ó Rathaille,

Michael Hartnett wrote no more poetry. On 13 October 1999 he died in St Vincent's Hospital in Dublin. He was laid to rest in the Calvary Cemetery in Newcastle West under a limestone cross carved by Cliodhna Cussen, depicting a necklace of wrens and bearing two lines from Michael's 1978 poem for his son Niall:

'Beadsa ann d'ainneoin an bháis
mar labhraíonn dúc is labhraíonn pár.'

'I will be there in spite of death
for ink speaks and paper speaks.'

['Dán do Niall, 7/Poem to Niall, 7']

On Sibelius's eighty-fifth birthday in 1950 the President of Finland motored out twenty miles from Helsinki to the composer's home in the countryside to pay the nation's respects. But when Michael Hartnett died the President of Ireland not only did not attend his funeral, but chose not to represent herself at it.

Such was the official view of a poet-scholar of our state and nation, in death as in life, except for one redeeming caveat. Just as the Finnish government in 1897 – mark you, 1897! – awarded Sibelius a state pension for life, likewise in 1981 the Taoiseach Mr Charles J. Haughey supported the setting up of Aosdána whereby the state offered a measure of financial support to artists who had made 'an outstanding contribution to the arts', foremost among them Michael Hartnett. Apart from the companionship of Angela Liston, had it not been for that financial support from the state in the shape of Aosdána, Michael Hartnett would have died long years before he did and we would never have had the great, rich and strange poems of his last period such as his *Sibelius in Silence*.

The Hartnett of *Sibelius in Silence* is of the stature of Cézanne or Cavafy and I repudiate the myth of him as a *petit maître local*. I repudiate the myth of him as the performing chimpanzee of the bar stools, a myth which is the creation of those suburban commissars who forty years ago in the 1960s and 1970s had it in their power to give a dazzling young scholar-poet support but who scorned him with snobbery, ignorance and neglect. I am glad to report that I feel exuberantly and unrepentantly bitter at what they did to Michael Hartnett and I hope I always will feel so. To the memory of my dead friend and comrade, in the solitude of my own fate, I raise my trembling glass.

A transcript of a lecture given in Trinity College Dublin, on 15 February 2006.

The Mystery of Harry Clifton

This is your saving grace – to restore mystery
To a common weal, and resurrect from disgrace
The non-political, kneeling in the unity
Of a moment's prayer …

[Harry Clifton, 'Death of Thomas Merton']

In 1994 I was invited by its editor Niall MacMonagle to write a foreword
to *Lifelines 2*, the astutely entitled anthology of favourite poems selected,
so the subtitle stated, by 'famous people' in replies to letters of invita-
tion from students of Wesley College, Dublin. In the course of reading
a proof copy I came upon a poem which I had never read before and
which startled me in a way which does not happen often to me when
reading contemporary verse. The poem was entitled 'Vaucluse' and the
name at the bottom of the poem was Harry Clifton. Not for the first
time in my life I was puzzled by that name.

Like anyone else, I dare say, who has lived their life in and around
Irish poetry, the name Harry Clifton was a name I was familiar with
since boyhood; since about the age of fifteen when I read W. B. Yeats's
late poem 'Lapis Lazuli' which begins with a dedication in parenthesis
'(For Harry Clifton)'. Yeats's poem had been published in *New Poems* in
1938 and therefore the author of 'Vaucluse' could hardly be the same
Harry Clifton as the dedicatee of 'Lapis Lazuli'. But it was just about
possible. Or maybe he was a son. Or grandson. It seemed unlikely that,
within the arena of Irish poetry, there were two Harry Cliftons belonging
to separate and unconnected families. A biographical note at the back
of *Lifelines 2* gave 1952 as the date of Harry Clifton's birth so a son or

grandson seemed a credible explanation. I marvelled at the conjunction that the author of this startling poem 'Vaucluse' was the descendant of the dedicatee of 'Lapis Lazuli'.

I did not know Harry Clifton in 1994 nor had I ever met anyone who knew him. I formed an impression that he lived and worked in far-off distant lands in Africa and Asia. The sparse biographical information seemed fitting for one who was a descendant of the dedicatee of 'Lapis Lazuli' with its universal, sweeping evocations of other lands, other eras, other civilisations:

> On their own feet they came, or on shipboard,
> Camel-back, horse-back, ass-back, mule-back,
> Old civilisations put to the sword.
> Then they and their wisdom went to rack ...

About the Harry Clifton to whom 'Lapis Lazuli' was dedicated I had never read nor heard anything since first reading the poem thirty-five years earlier and while I realised that it was impossible that he and the author of 'Vaucluse' were one and the same person, the nagging feeling persisted that they *were* one and the same person.

What I wish to attempt now is to think aloud about that first reading in 1994 of the poem entitled 'Vaucluse' and my subsequent readings of it down thirteen years and about how that poem led me into reading all the rest of Harry Clifton's poetry and prose culminating in a second reading experience in 2006, which, in the manner in which it startled me, was a comparable experience to reading 'Vaucluse' in 1994. In January 2006 while I was posted in Trinity College Dublin, Dr Philip Coleman one day left for me in the office of the School of English a large envelope (the sort used for mailing poster-size photographs); it contained a lettered (H) and signed copy of a broadsheet published by Dr Coleman under the imprint KORE BROADSHEETS # 10 which reproduced a poem by Harry Clifton entitled 'Benjamin Fondane Departs for the East'.

'Vaucluse' was submitted to the *Lifelines 2* anthology by the novelist Deirdre Madden, with the accompanying letter addressed to three Wesley College students:

Dear Ewan, Aine and Christopher:
 My favourite poem is 'Vaucluse', by my husband Harry Clifton. It relates to a time before we were married, when I was spending some months in the south of France, and Harry came out to visit me. We went to Aix-en-Provence together, and to Marseilles. It's a marvellous poem, and it means a great deal to me.
 Good luck with 'Lifelines'.
 All best wishes
 Deirdre Madden

Vaucluse

Cognac, like a gold sun
Blazed in me, turning
The landscape inside out –
I had left the South
An hour ago, and the train
Through Arles, through Avignon,
Fed on electricity
Overhead, and quickened my mind
With infinite platforms, cypress trees,
Stone villages, the granaries
Of Provence, and I saw again
France, like a blue afternoon
Genius makes hay in, and drink improves –
The worked fields, the yellow sheaves
In shockwaves, perceived
And lit from within, by love.

By then, I suppose,
You had made your own connections,
My chance, eventual girl,
And half Marseilles had closed
For the hot hours – the awnings of cafés
With nothingness in their shadows,
And the drink put away
For another day
Not ours ...
                    I see, I remember
Coldly now, as I see ourselves
And the merchants from Africa, glozening
Liquor on the shelves
Of celebration, everyone dozing
In transmigratory dreams
Of heroin, garlic and cloves –
And how we got there, you and I,
By trade route or intuition, seems,
Like charts for sale on the Occident streets,
As fabulous, as obsolete
As a map of the known world.

But then again, how kind he was,
The dark *patron* ... and it lasted,
That shot of cognac,
An hour, till the train
Occluded in grey rain
Above Lyons, and the Rhone Valley
Darkened. I would carry
Your books, your winter clothes
Through stations, streets of Paris
To a cold repose
In the North. We would meet again
In months to come, and years,

Exchanging consciousness, reason, and tears
Like beggars. Transfigured,
Not yet fallen from grace
I saw us, not as we are
But new in love, in the hallowed place
Of sources, the sacred fountains
Of Petrarch and René Char.

'Vaucluse' is first a love poem, secondly a train poem, thirdly a North and South of France poem. It consists of three passages of mostly short, three-stress lines. The phrase 'love poem' trips lightly off the tongue, but in the reality of literature an authentic love poem is a rare occurrence. Look at the last hundred years of Irish literature and how many authentic love poems will you come up with? Rarer still are poems of married love, which this poem also is. The moment, which is the occasion of the poem, happens only once or twice in a lifetime and to catch it is almost impossible. Usually the writer winds up with a wodge of rhetoric dangling from a fork; memorable rhetoric sometimes but merely rhetoric. In the rat race of *ersatz* romance, an authentic love poem is a strange item.

The poem takes its title from the department in the South of France, one of the departments of Provence. Vaucluse is so-named after the village of Fontaine-de-Vaucluse, the ancient Vallis Clausa or 'Fountain of the Enclosed Valley' of Roman times. The 'fountain' of Vaucluse is claimed to be the deepest spring well in the world. Lying under a 230-metre-high cliff at the top of what in the days before tourism was a secluded valley, the green spring can be docile or turbulent. In the first century AD Seneca wrote of it: 'Where the impetuous torrent escapes from the abyss, the spring is sacred because of the unfathomable depth of its waters.' The spring of Vaucluse is a kind of Provençal Delphi. Its waters form the source of the River Sorgue, which flows through the old town of L'Isle-sur-la-Sorgue, birthplace and home of the poet René Char. The glorious climax of Harry Clifton's poem sings of:

> ... the hallowed place
> Of sources, the sacred fountains
> Of Petrarch and René Char.

A presiding genius of the first passage is Vincent Van Gogh and one feels that the poet has specific paintings of Van Gogh in mind: *A Cornfield, with Cypresses* and *Midday, after Millet.* The reader is brought face to face with those unmistakeable corrugations of paint on the surface of canvas:

> The worked fields, the yellow sheaves
> In shockwaves, perceived
> And lit from within, by love.

I get the impression also of the poet co-opting Van Gogh in the making of the image of the train being 'Fed on electricity / Overhead'. That is a painting that Vincent did not himself get to make but it is one which in Clifton's poem he is brought back to make. I can see in that first passage the bent figure of Van Gogh in a field near Arles painting the train from Marseilles as it flashes past. Having trudged through the Francis Bacon painting (*Study for a Portrait of Van Gogh IV*, 1957), he is presently ensconced on the edge of the Clifton poem. A second presiding genius of the first passage is the eighteenth-century Irish philosopher George Berkeley whose central tenet of *esse est percipi* lies behind its lines.

The image of the train is vital to the poem as it is vital to all Clifton's work. The train in Clifton is a pre-lapsarian form of transport; so pre-lapsarian as if to seem an essential fixture of the furniture of the Garden of Eden. Trains in Clifton play a life-changing role: at once life-enhancing and life-destroying. The train seems to create the very world it is flashing through. The train splashes 'infinite platforms' on the canvas; the train throws up the very cypress trees it is shooting past; the train conjures up vistas of infinity – 'infinite platforms'. The poet announces that he has 'left the South' and we are left in no doubt by the end of the poem that the south is the equivalent of the Garden of Eden. Ironically the electricity of the train and its overhead wires are taking him northward darkly and away from the blue south and all its electric connections of love.

In the second passage the poet sketches the woman of the poem, the beloved, the bride-to-be whom he depicts in those four chosen words 'My chance, eventual girl'. In the cold light of sitting alone on the train speeding north, he recalls their meeting of only an hour or two previously; their having a drink together in a café in Marseilles. He tells us of 'the shelves of celebration', reminding us in our illness-beset culture in the north of the original purpose of alcohol which is to celebrate life, not destroy it. He imagines her now back in Marseilles in the hot hours and 'the awnings of cafés / With nothingness in their shadows'. A sculpted, pictorial image, a fusion of de Staël and Cézanne. He speaks of 'everyone dozing in transmigratory dreams' as if to suggest that the true element of humanity is the journey and the cosmos, not the static and the provincial. And he asks that question that all lovers finally cannot help but ask: by the power of what obscure agency did they have the good fortune to meet? Was it indeed good fortune or was it some kind of pre-ordained destiny, some form of providence?

The third and final passage of the triptych portrays the deity as being a 'dark *patron*' who is benign. By now the train has been travelling northward for an hour and it is past Lyons. In a sculpted, linguistic image the train is depicted as darkening after having been 'Occluded in grey rain'. This is the darkness of the north, a radically other darkness to that of the shadows in Marseilles in the mid-afternoon. We learn that the narrator is carrying the books and winter clothes of the beloved to Paris in the cold north. A Rembrandt-like image of the beloved; she is her books, she is her winter clothes. Marriage is prefigured and defined as a state of 'Exchanging consciousness, reason and tears / Like beggars.' What an astounding image. Could it also be out of Rembrandt? *The Jewish Bride*?

We come to the climax of the poem. The transfiguration of the pair of lovers in Fontaine-de-Vaucluse and the invocation of the names of

Petrarch and René Char. In depicting the transfiguration by love, Clifton adumbrates a theology of original sin; as we are, we are fallen; as transfigured by love, we are new. In these lines he achieves both a Camus-like lucidity as in *The First Man* and the innocence of Dylan Thomas's 'Fern Hill'. When I first read the last lines thirteen years ago, those two names, Petrarch and René Char, carried a powerful charge as they were meant to do and the strange fact of poetry and life is that after all these years they continue to carry that charge.

Petrarch. The fourteenth-century poet of love who lived part of his early life in Avignon and later in Fontaine-de-Vaucluse 'on the left bank of the Sorgue' as he tells us and in whose poetry are to be found images of the 'Fountain of the Enclosed Valley'. He was, as well as being a poet, a humanist and scholar which is pertinent when we consider the intellectual basis of the lyricism of Harry Clifton; and he saw himself as a permanent dissident and exile everywhere (*'peregrinus ubique'*). Like Clifton, Petrarch believed a poet can be at home only in exile.

The copper-fastening name is that of René Char who spent a lifetime tracing the abyss of the mystery at the fountain of Vaucluse: 'poetry', he wrote 'is, of all clear waters, the least likely to linger at the reflection of its bridges' (quoted in Caws, *René Char*). The name of René Char tastes of the Resistance, the *maquis*, rugby football and lyric poetry and it evokes the landscape of Provence in the area of the Vaucluse; that bare, mountainous, red landscape under blue skies. It's a name that also brings back to mind instantaneously the names of Martin Heidegger and Albert Camus; those lost worlds that are none the less real for being lost; maybe the more real for being lost.

In the story of my own life, it was in the early 1960s in connection with Heidegger that I first came upon the tracks of the poet René Char; Heidegger who, invoking the pre-Socratic philosophers asked the same question that haunts the poetry of Harry Clifton: how should we dwell on earth? In the 1950s the disgraced German philosopher found a friend and disciple in the person of René Char. Heidegger, castigated for his dealings with the Nazi regime, found a sympathetic, congenial sanctuary in the Vaucluse in René Char, culminating in the legendary seminars at Le Thor. Char was as renowned for his exploits as a Resistance leader as for his poetry; the 'Capitaine Alexandre' of Resistance mythology. Later in reading of Albert Camus I came upon René Char again. Camus had come to know René Char in 1945 and he revered Char both as a poet and as a friend.

Twelve years later in 2006 I read for the first time Harry Clifton's poem 'Benjamin Fondane Departs for the East'.

Look at us now, from the vanished years –
      Paris between the wars.
Penelopes and Juliets, pimps and racketeers
Of sugar and tobacco. Boys and girls
With stars on their lapels, who sleep on straw
Like everyone else, and carry out the slops.
And who could deny we're equals, under a Law
Annihilating us all? Conformists, resisters,
You I would never abandon, my own soul-sister,
Drinking brassy water from the taps

Of Drancy, where time and space are the antechamber
      To our latest idea of eternity –
Trains going east in convoys, sealed and numbered,
To an unknown destination, *Pitchipoi*
As the wits describe it, after the Yiddish tale –
A village in a clearing, zlotys changed for francs,
Children at their books, the old and frail
Looked after, and the rest suspiciously blank
On the postcards drifting like dead leaves
Back from that other world we are asked to believe in.

Death is not absolute! Two and two make five!
      My poems will survive!

Why not fly in the face of reason and scream
As Shestov says? Unscramble the anagram
Of my real name, which now is mud,
And tell Jean Wahl and Bachelard, *bien pensants*,
I forgive them, as they stalk the corridors
Of the Sorbonne, and the pages of the *Cahiers du Sud*.
I forgive them, for they know not who they are.
Irrational, fleeting, caught between wars,

Faking their own death, in thirteen nation-states,
        As the monies collapse
And the borders, and everyone transmigrates
Like souls, through the neutral space on the maps.
Athens and Jerusalem, Ulysses and the Wandering Jew –
There they all go, the living, the dead,
The one in the other ... Call them the Paris Crowd,
Unreal, uprooted, spectres drifting through,
The ashes of their ancestors in suitcases,
Bound for Buenos Aires, bound for the New.

In the steamroom dissipatings, the bathhouse stink,
        As the people of the Book
Undressed themselves, I learned at last how to think.
I saw the shame and beauty, and I shook
At patriarchs' aged knees, the love-handles of hips
And women's breasts, emerging, disappearing,
Standing, kneeling, waiting, finally stripped
Of civilisation – in their natural state.
At the heart of the orgy, I saw into the years
Beyond steam and faucets to the real Apocalypse.

And now they tell me 'Hide your poems, wait –
        Somewhere in Nineteen Eighty
Readers will find you ...' I see a Paris street,

Old letterbox, a drop-zone for the infinite
In a leaf-littered hallway, where a publisher long ago
Went out of business, and a young man searches
In the sibylline mess and the overflow
For a few lost words – my own soul-sister, my wife
Till death do us part, in the Eastern Marches –
And that, who knows, will be the afterlife.

The text is followed by a brief, italicised biographical note:

Romanian Jewish poet Benjamin Fondane (1898–1944), moved to Paris in 1923. Deported from Drancy, he died in Birkenau.

The title 'Benjamin Fondane Departs for the East' reads as a kind of public announcement at which the reader is invited to behold and participate in the spectacle – *spectacle* in the French sense of the phrase – of a Romanian-Jewish poet being deported by train from a suburban railway station, Drancy, near Paris to his incarceration and death in the concentration camp at Auschwitz-Birkenau in Poland in 1944. The title has a news-desk, circus ring to it. It carries within itself the incantatory note of ringmaster and newsreel commentator. 'Hurry up folks, gather round, stop press. Benjamin Fondane departs for the East. Right now. Get your tickets. Roll up and watch him. Watch his departure. Come along now. Hurry up.'

The poet in the first line assumes the voice of Fondane himself and in that voice, sustaining it throughout the poem, he paints for us scenes of the Holocaust particular to him and his family, yet applicable to the entire Jewish race.

The voice is daring, insouciant, oracular, almost but not quite arrogant. He invites us to look, and by implication stare at him and his family and his people in their hour of maximum humiliation, anguish and degradation. His tone is mocking, gossipy, resigned, bitter, ironic. A gay spirit in the face of evil. 'Gaiety transfiguring all that dread.' He is sparklingly bitter and passionately ironic. The poem is an elegy, a declaration, a harangue, a wisdom-poem, a confession, a credo, a performance, above all, first and last, a cry, an articulate cry from the heart. It is a painting by, all at once, Chagall, Soutine and Jankel Adler.

The poem is comprised of six ten-line stanzas and in the opening stanza the voice of Fondane summons us to the world of 'Paris between the wars', 1918–39, the world of '*l'entre deux guerres*' as recalled by Eliot in 'East Coker', the ghettos where boys and girls 'sleep on straw ... and carry out the slops'. In the tone of Pushkin throwing down a challenge, Fondane launches a rhetorical question in a rant of scorn: 'And who could deny we're equals, under a Law / Annihilating us all?' Then he turns away from us, his audience, and addresses his sister, Lina, who was arrested with him on 7 March 1944 and whom Fondane was invited by his captors to abandon in exchange for his own freedom. He refused to abandon his sister whom Clifton portrays for us in an image of great tenderness as she drinks water from the taps, the 'brassy water' as he puts it, of Drancy.

The second stanza opens with another outburst of sarcasm in which Fondane describes Drancy as being the place 'where time and space are the antechamber / To our latest idea of eternity'. This modish idea is embodied in the form of 'trains going east in convoys'. His black humour deepens as he recounts how postcards used to arrive in Drancy from the east with pictures of children at kindergarten and the aged in retirement and with lots of blank space around the illustrations. In Drancy people used to joke about these postcards and they used to say how they came from a place called 'Pitchipoi', a fabled village paradise in Yiddish folklore that might have come straight out of a Chagall painting or an Isaac Babel story.

The third stanza opens with assertions of controlled, rhyming hysteria. 'Death is not absolute! Two and two make five! / My poems will survive!' We the readers are made to feel that the speaker regards these assertions as being at once true and ludicrous. Fondane invokes the name of Lev Shestov (1866–1938), the Russian-Jewish philosopher who was a dominant, controversial figure in the intelligentsia in Paris between the wars and whose credo proclaimed the futility of reason and the primacy of feeling. The speaker in the poem cries: 'Why not fly in the face of reason and scream / As Shestov says?' In his fury, almost mumbling to himself and flying in the face of reason, Fondane tells us he will drop his pseudonym or as he puts it, 'unscramble the anagram / Of my real name'.

Fondane was born Benjamin Wechsler in 1898 in Jassy in Moldavia in what is now the north-east of Romania. His uncles and his maternal grandfather were eminent Jewish intellectuals. Six languages were spoken in his home: Romanian, German, French, English, Yiddish and Hebrew. At the age of fourteen, he published poems under the name of Benjamin Fundoianu, taking his pen-name from the name of the countryside of his paternal ancestors. In Paris to which he emigrated in 1923 the Romanian Fundoianu became the French Fondane. Addressing the philosophers Jean Wahl and Gaston Bachelard, Fondane haughtily tells us that he forgives them. What is it he is forgiving them? Their rationalism; their being establishment stalwarts, sensible '*bien pensants*'. Fondane, in the manner of the Clifton of 'Vaucluse', dips his pen in the aura and romance of proper names, of 'the Sorbonne and the pages of the *Cahiers du Sud*'.

The poem is constructed like an Irish high cross with each stanza a discrete panel depicting a different episode of the Holocaust while the narrative thread of Fondane's voice weaves its fierce, delicate interleave. The fourth stanza is a picture of what Clifton calls 'the Paris Crowd', the heart of the Jewish diaspora exiled and drifting in Europe and beyond. Again that signature Clifton word, 'transmigrates', and the conflation of economics, politics, geography, anthropology and history: 'and everyone transmigrates / Like souls, through the neutral space on maps'. Again the invocation and romance of proper names: 'Athens and Jerusalem, Ulysses and the Wandering Jew'. These refer also to the major book-titles of Fondane's life; the title of Shestov's magnum opus, *Athens and Jerusalem* (1938) and the title of Fondane's own magnum opus 'Ulysses' (1933), which in his private shorthand he referred to as 'the Wandering Jew'. Echoes of Baudelaire and Eliot from 'Les Sept Vieillards' and from *The Waste Land*: 'Fourmillante cité, cité pleine de rêves / Où le spectre en plein jour raccroche le passant!': 'Unreal City / Under the brown fog of a winter dawn'; 'There they all go, the living and the dead / The one in the other ... Call them the Paris Crowd / Unreal, uprooted'. Here we are locked into the nightmare world of the stateless immigrant, the torment of being an alien at everyone's mercy, the bureaucratic inferno of work permits, ration coupons and identity cards. Alluding to Fondane's own voyages to Argentina in 1929 and 1936, the speaker in the poem sees these apparitions as 'spectres drifting through, / The ashes of their ancestors in suitcases, / Bound for Buenos Aires'. As well the felicitous rhyming of 'suitcases' with 'Buenos Aires', we may note the partial transcription of one of the opening lines of Fondane's poem 'Ulysses' dedicated to his brother-in-law Armand Pascal: 'Armand your ashes weigh so heavily in my suitcase'. 'Bound for Buenos Aires' is also, I surmise, an evocation of Witold Gombrowicz who escaped to Buenos Aires (by mistake!) in 1939 and who, I believe, is a tutelary antecedent of Clifton's.

In the fifth stanza we arrive at the nadir of the Holocaust, but at the zenith of Fondane's own perception of it as understood and communicated by Clifton. Fondane asserts that only by travelling into this ultimate debacle did he become capable of thinking for himself. This is a catastrophic claim. For it was in philosophy that Fondane had been primarily engaged in the journals and halls of Paris in the 1920s and 1930s. He was the epitome of the poet-philosopher. Along with his teacher and mentor Shestov he had come to form the leading prong of attack on one side of the intense debate between religious existentialism and secular rationalism. In Clifton's poem, Fondane is echoing Simone Weil: 'You could not be born at a better period than the present, when we have lost everything' (Weil, *Gravity and Grace*, p. 156).

In the fifth stanza we see again in Clifton's technique the emergence of the sensibility of Rembrandt. For who else but Rembrandt could be behind these lines in which Fondane reports how, having arrived at the concentration camp, he 'shook / At patriarchs' aged knees, the love-handles of hips / And women's breasts, emerging, disappearing, / Standing, kneeling, waiting'. It is not seemly to dwell on images of private horror and desolation but in this instance it behoves us to repeat these words and consider them as we would stand before a picture by Rembrandt: 'and I shook / At patriarchs' aged knees, the love-handles of hips / And women's breasts, emerging, disappearing, / Standing, kneeling, waiting'. It behoves us to focus on that one phrase 'the love-handles of hips / And women's breasts' and ask ourselves where we might have seen this image before and by whose hand: 'the love-handles of hips / And women's breasts'.

But all that sacred delft and holy hardware of God's creation is, in the concentration camp, about to be 'finally stripped / Of civilisation'. This is 'the heart of the orgy'. This is what happens in concentration camps; and, Fondane had argued for twenty years, in social structures of the modern era, in their systematic, mechanical, totally impersonal materialism. The 'people of the Book' are treated not as the people of the Book but as fuel of the Political Machine and the Abstract Idea; not with respect but with hateful contempt.

In the sixth and final stanza Fondane considers what being a poet may have meant to him and what may be meant by the concept of 'the afterlife', if anything; by such notions as 'fame' and 'immortality'. He is vouchsafed a glimpse into the future, into the 1980s – forty years after his death – and he sees a nondescript street in Paris and the office of a defunct publisher in whose letter box a young man seeking after poetry comes upon wind-blown copies of Fondane's own poems. The last line reads: 'And that, who knows, will be the afterlife.' The letter box, 'a drop-zone for the infinite', is located in a 'leaf-littered hallway'. Are poems also, it is being asked, like the dead leaves of postcards from Pitchipoi/ Auschwitz drifting 'back from that other world we are asked to believe in'?

So that is what it may mean to have been a poet. To have lived your life in obscurity, a kind of hiding one's life away on the basis of a weird faith that sometime after your death, say forty or fifty years after your death, there is the possibility that some young man lost in his own journey may unearth your poems – 'a few lost words' – and bring them to light.

The tone of voice in the poem is the key to the author's sense of Fondane. It is an outraged voice, an audacious voice, an angry voice, a non-conformist voice. And when you look at Fondane's life story, at the totality of it, at all forty-six years of it, you see that that is what above all else he was: a non-conformist. In 1916 at the age of eighteen the precocious young Jew wrote: 'And I wept in the Garden of Gethsemane and I died on the Cross and I rose from the dead not on the third day but in the souls of those who understood me' ('Métempsychose'). Already a modernist as an adolescent in the Romanian provinces before the First World War; a high modernist, Francophile, dissident in Bucharest in the years after the First World War; an exile in Paris from 1923 until his murder in 1944.

In Paris Fondane not only stood at the cutting edge of philosophy and poetry, he was ahead of the cutting edge. He was the avant-garde of the avant-garde. From early on in Paris, he was out there with Picabia, Brancusi, Man Ray, Artaud, Tzara. For him the central, fundamental fact of human existence was the absurdity of death. He was the archetypal Romanian-Jewish émigré and, in the photographs that survive of him, he looks the part; gay, handsome, laughing, intellectual; enormous, arched, black eyebrows; wide, glittering eyes; cigarette dangling from the corner of the mouth; jacket draped over the shoulders; multicoloured scarf. There is a marvellous photograph from 1938 of Fondane with his wife Geneviève Tissier in which both of them are sparkling with the joy of life.

For Fondane the cinema was where it was at in art; and the cinema at its purest for him was by definition surrealist. In poetry his hero was Rimbaud. His first book of poems in French, published in 1928 with a photograph by Man Ray, was entitled *Cinépoêmes*.

In 1931 the Argentinian woman of letters Victoria Ocampo founded the journal *Sur*, a cosmopolitan journal of art and literature, based in Buenos Aires. She published Fondane from 1931 to 1940. She arranged for him to visit Buenos Aires in 1929 and 1936 to present avant-garde films and to participate in conferences. These three-week voyages across the Atlantic Ocean by way of Dakar and Rio de Janeiro were of massive importance in Fondane's life as a poet, providing him with material for his epic poem 'Ulysses'. Another source of inspiration was Tennyson's poem 'Ulysses' written in 1833:

> To follow knowledge like a sinking star
> Beyond the utmost bound of human thought.

Such are the consanguinities that lift poetry to its proper level in the human story; from a twenty-first-century suburban-raised Irishman to a vagabond twentieth-century Romanian Jew to a nineteenth-century, lordly, English poet laureate.

With the Occupation of Paris in 1940 Fondane became nonchalant. When the Germans ordered that Jews wear yellow stars on their lapels, he ignored the order. His friends marvelled at his big, warm voice greeting them in the streets with his trademark *'Alors*, what's the news?' To a nosey baroness at a literary party he announced *'Je suis Victor Hugo.'* On 7 March 1944, betrayed by his concierge, he was arrested along with his sister Lina and taken to the prefecture at Île de la Cité. Having refused the offer of freedom to stay by the side of his sister he was deported from Drancy to Auschwitz-Birkenau on 30 May 1944. He had four months to live. The choice he was forced into making in Drancy, a choice not only between life and death, but between his sister and his wife, Clifton transmutes into an almost unbearably tender image of Fondane making his sister his bride. In Clifton's poem Fondane suddenly turns to his sister and addresses her as 'my own soul-sister, my wife / Till death do us part, in the Eastern Marches'.

Witnesses have testified how Fondane ran a kind of literary salon in Auschwitz. In a corner of a bunkhouse, although ill and weak and singled out by the *capos* for derision and mockery, Fondane regaled his comrades with memories of Paris in the 1920s and with readings from his epic poem 'Ulysses'. The doctor who attended him, Lazar Moscovici, wrote of how Fondane's 'warm voice was that of the fireside storytellers of old in Romania dazzling children with the wonders of tales of fairies and dragons'. Moscovici tells us how 'in the evenings of the last weeks of his life Fondane recited his poem "Ulysses" which had become an elegy for the Jewish race and which symbolised his fate. And with what tenderness he spoke to us of his wife Geneviève, of his own den in Paris, of his books and his paintings ... of brotherhood and humanity.'

On the morning of 2 October 1944, in freezing rain, Fondane was loaded onto a lorry to take him to his death. The philosopher and fellow-countryman of Fondane, E. Cioran wrote: '... Fondane was resigned to his lot ... there was in him a peculiar complicity with the inevitable ... only this can explain his refusal to take any precaution, of which the rudimentary would have been to change his country of residence ...' This testimony is in accord with all we know of Fondane's heroic, casual attitude to life. But Cioran also added:

> Fondane was a superior man. Someone noble, above ordinary things. He refused to abandon Lina and accept his liberation. He had risen above normal miseries: as a man he was superior to Man. He had gone beyond the world in his own career, without pride or demonstrativeness – he was incapable of that. He was a man set apart, by that extraordinary nobility ... (quoted in Clifton, 'Shylock's lament')

In other words, it might be proper to ascribe to Fondane something of the sanctity of known martyrs such as Bonhoeffer. Probably Fondane would have eschewed the term 'sanctity' but as we see and hear and witness him in Clifton's poem we are encouraged and permitted to ascribe to him the mysterious condition of sanctity.

When Fondane died at the hands of the Nazis his poetry died with him and it was to be fifty years before his *Collected Poems* were published in Paris in 1996 and in 2004 a critical biography, *Benjamin Fondane* by Olivier Salazar-Ferrer. In 1993, in Kfar-Saba in Israel, the inauguration took place of the Society for Benjamin Fondane Studies. Such is 'the afterlife' of the poet.

The reader will bring to Clifton's poem his or her own knowledge of Fondane. In my own case I became aware of Benjamin Fondane in 1965 in London when in David Gascoyne's *Collected Poems* (1965) I read his 1942 poem 'To Benjamin Fondane'. This is a matter of significance to me because I can see in Fondane an antecedent of Gascoyne, the visionary English poet, visionary in the mystic pieties of Samuel Palmer as well as in the revelations of Blake and Hölderlin. In 1986 the magazine *Aquarius* published Gascoyne's essay 'Meetings with Benjamin Fondane'.

In 1978 I met Francis Stuart for the first time and not long after in one of numerous conversations with him from 1978 until 2000, the year of his death, Francis Stuart cited to me the name of Benjamin Fondane as being one of the – for him – significant figures of European literature. Fondane was possibly an unofficial member of Stuart's own pantheon, which he called 'the High Consistory', although Fondane does not feature in Stuart's novel of that name. Fondane does, however, feature in an earlier Stuart novel, *The Pillar of Cloud* (1948). In an essay on Fondane in 2005 in the *Dublin Review* Harry Clifton remarks on the poignant significance of Stuart being a primary transmitter, so to speak, in the English language of Fondane.

That Fondane, a Jewish martyr of the Holocaust, was close to Stuart's heart and that Stuart featured him in his novel and translated his poetry are heartbreaking facts when one recalls the abuse heaped on Stuart for his alleged Nazi sympathies. The fact of the matter is that Stuart, like Fondane and Gascoyne and Clifton, is a diasporist in all things; that outsiderness might be described as the Jewish aspect of Stuart.

Taking together the two poems, 'Vaucluse' and 'Benjamin Fondane Departs for the East' we see that both poems are based on a train journey; the one representing the journey from and into all that is good in this life, the journey made under the sign of love; the other, a journey into the heart of evil, made under the sign of extraordinary courage; the one sings of the beatific fountains of the Enclosed Valley, the other depicts the vile fountains of the gas chambers of Auschwitz; both poems evoke and invoke the lives of poets; both poems put a value on poetry in the affairs of mankind. Each poem is driven by a specific energy: 'Vaucluse' by the energy of love; and 'Benjamin Fondane Departs for the East' by the energy of anger. In another poem of married love,

'The Liberal Cage', originally published in 1988 alongside 'Vaucluse', Clifton had written:

> But listen ... not in doubt,
> Contentment, or in pure mind,
> But in anger alone, will we find
> The key that lets us out.

Part of the mystery of Harry Clifton is how and why a child of post-war Ireland, a child of the middle-class, garden suburbs of post-war Dublin took it upon himself to speak in the person of a Romanian-Jewish intellectual who was born more than an hundred years ago in Moldavia and, in doing so in the form of a poem in the English language, succeeded in catching the authentic voice of the Romanian Jew. The obstacles to such an achievement may be gauged by considering the 1982 sculpture of James Joyce, a contemporary of Fondane's, outside the Newman Building in University College Dublin. Apparently Joyce, it is more a representation of a Trotskyite militiaman than of Joyce whereas Clifton's Fondane is carved from inside the soul of the man as he stands among the charnel houses of the European nightmare. Clifton has depicted both the spiritual reality of Fondane's personality as well as the circumstance of his tragedy. Whereas Joe McCaul the Irish sculptor of the Irishman Joyce has not experienced Joyce, the Irishman Clifton has experienced the Romanian-Jewish Fondane and, by his success in entering into his subjectivity, communicated him to us in the music of his poetry. The seeds of Clifton's achievement were sown thirty years earlier when in his master's thesis ('Imaginative Absolute in Wallace Stevens') he investigated Hume's theory of imagination 'as *sympathy* where the imagination translates an idea into an impression in order to participate sympathetically in the experience of another' (Clifton, cf. Hume, *A Treatise of Human Nature*, pp 385–6). Clifton followed up his 1975 research with an apprenticeship of thirty years in writing poetry during which he sought to recreate the life-experiences of thinkers and poets, among them Thomas Merton, Dag Hammarskjöld, Hart Crane, Dostoyevsky, Silone, Kierkegaard, and Hopkins.

In 1987 in his Raven Arts Press pamphlet *Martyrs and Metaphors* Colm Tóibín momentarily illuminated Harry Clifton's suburban upbringing when he wrote (p. 16) that Clifton was 'brought up in the suburbs of Dublin: an Ireland which had no official recognition'. To be a child of the Dublin suburbs in the 1950s and 1960s was to be displaced, alien, disorientated, almost stateless.

Considering the œuvre of Harry Clifton in the light of 'Vaucluse' and 'Benjamin Fondane Departs for the East', seven volumes of poetry and two volumes of prose, not to mention multifarious fugitive publication in journals and newspapers, one is struck by the persistence of particular preoccupations.

First, there is Clifton's fascination with trains. It is there in his first volume of poems, published at the age of twenty-five, *The Walls of Carthage* (1977), in a poem entitled 'Two Stations in Paris' which constitute two still lifes of the Gare du Nord and the Gare St Lazare. Again an image of the overhead lines feeding electricity to the trains:

Blueprint of metal tangents – curving away
Into what human distance, separation pure
At the end of an alien day?

The ticket machine is seen as

    the photo-
Electric imprimatur

Of a passenger gate

A long-range snapshot sings of

Cantilevered sublime
Where everyone but the pigeons
Is an alien, and time
Is its own religion.

His sixth collection, *Night Train through the Brenner*, taking its title from an account of a train journey from Munich to Florence in 1989, contains the poem 'Watershed' which begins

>On the spine of Italy
>Our train had come to a standstill

It contains also 'The Marriage Feast', a magical poem linking the marriage process to that sacramental moment in a railway station when the uncoupling of carriages and the switching of tracks takes place.

Secondly, there is Clifton's obsession with Europe's primary sources and forgotten beginnings; its water tables and watersheds being keened over, one is made to feel, by Heraclitus and Parmenides as well as by René Char and Petrarch. Physical health, spiritual health, Clifton seems to be reminding us, are one and the same and they will be rediscovered only in the sources of primeval Europe and not in the artificial spas of megasonic wealth and so, in 'Taking the Waters', he writes:

>There are taps that flow, all day and all night,
>From the depths of Europe,
>Inexhaustible, taken for granted,
>
>Slaking our casual thirsts
>At a railway station
>Heading south, or here in the Abruzzo
>
>Bursting cold from an iron standpipe
>While our blind mouths
>Suck at essentials, straight from the water table.
>[…]
>History passes, only the waters remain,
>
>Bubbling up, through their carbon sheets,
>To the other side of catastrophe
>Where we drink at a forgotten source,

[80]

Through the old crust of Europe
Centuries deep ...

The opening line of his 1994 poem 'Watershed', 'On the spine of Italy ...' gave Clifton the title of his prose journal of four seasons in a mountain-top village in the Abruzzi, which is also a chronicle of water and about water and to water, a narrative of snow and ice and melt-water and mountain torrents. In *On the Spine of Italy* water is physically omnipresent and the whole book bears out the truth of its epigraph, 'The greatest poverty is not to live / In a physical world', lines from Wallace Stevens's late poem 'Esthétique du Mal'.

Thirdly, there is the vision of woman as the beloved in 'Vaucluse' and 'Benjamin Fondane Departs for the East', which in the shadowy, shuttered world of call-girls and street-walkers in his earlier books is tantamount to a tearing apart of the curtains at dawn to reveal the transfigured person. In the earlier books woman is either inaccessible self-containment or a 'monsoon girl' in a brothel delineated in what in *The Field Day Anthology of Irish Writing* (1991), Declan Kiberd described as Clifton's 'distinctive, personal fever and chill'.

Into this cityscape of sexual estrangement, 'Vaucluse' and 'Benjamin Fondane Departs for the East' burst like *aislings*. In 'Vaucluse', transfigured by love, the woman becomes a real person, 'my chance, eventual girl', and in 'Benjamin Fondane Departs for the East' there is the exquisite idea of the bride as 'soul-sister'. Back in 1988, 'Vaucluse' released in Clifton's poetry fountains of spousal love. In 2003 in his book *God in France*, there is a short poem entitled 'Bare Arm' in which we observe two strangers, a married woman and a married man, glimpse one another in dormer windows in the roof-tops of Paris. It is a sort of Edward Hopper/Édouard Vuillard epiphany:

Naked, in the small hours,
Coming from showers
And lovemaking, two spouses
In opposite houses

[81]

Pausing, in the lit frame
Of revelation,
Not knowing each other's name,
Uncaring, unconditional

For once, two creatures
Awake, while everyone slept,
Alive in the forest
Of second nature

Fourthly, throughout Clifton's work one is conscious of the presence of Rembrandt. This is not surprising if we consider his short story 'The Rembrandt Series', a portrait of a Dublin civil servant in love for a lifetime with Rembrandt.

Lastly there is Clifton's golden obsession with Paris, as seen in his *Secular Eden: Paris Notebooks 1994–2004* (2007). In 2005 in his volume entitled *Harbour Lights* Derek Mahon published a poem with the same title as Yeats's poem of 1938 'Lapis Lazuli' and employing the same rubric of dedication as Yeats had employed sixty-seven years earlier: a name in parenthesis and that name being Harry Clifton.

(For Harry Clifton)

Once again we are jolted by the mystery of Harry Clifton. We are confronted also in the first lines of Mahon's poem with a chunk of lapis lazuli sitting on the poet's desk, 'a complex chunk … night-formed in sun-struck Afghanistan … A royal blue loved since the earth began / because, like the swirling sea, it never dates.' At the end of the second stanza Mahon hints at the identity of the Harry Clifton of his dedication. He writes:

Dim in the half-light of conventional rain
We start at the squeal of Berkeley's telephone.

The Hercule Poirot antennae of the alert, cultured reader will recall the publication in 2000 by the Lilliput Press of the volume *Berkeley's Telephone and Other Fictions*. The alert, cultured reader will also by this stage have read the second volume of Roy Foster's biography of W. B. Yeats in which we learn that the Harry Clifton to whom Yeats dedicated his poem was a poet also but that he was born in 1907, the son of Talbot and Violet Clifton, and died in 1978. His three volumes of verse were entitled *Dielma and Other Poems* (1932), *Flight* (1934) and *Gleams Britain's Day* (1942). The alert, cultured reader finally will have learned from the Christmas 2006 edition of the journal *Irish Pages* that the Harry Clifton of 'Vaucluse' and 'Benjamin Fondane Departs for the East' had for his mother a South American woman of Chilean extraction while his father was a migrant Irishman of Fenian, republican background.

In the concluding stanza of Mahon's poem we are vouchsafed a glimpse of a young woman on the Eurostar, the London–Paris train, a vignette we might expect to find in a Harry Clifton poem, and she is in the act of reading a book. The poet, offering to us an image of her book as a slate of lapis lazuli, portrays her as she searches its pages

... for the rich and rare.
Hope lies with her as it always does really
And the twinkling sages in the Deux Magots
First glimpsed by a student forty years ago
On a continent like a plain of lapis lazuli
And the Eurostar glides into the Gare du Nord.

Gare du Nord was the name also of the white rabbit beloved of Francis Stuart whose first wife was a young woman in whom W. B. Yeats had a certain interest; pieces of a patchwork mystery familiar to Mahon. And is Mahon also sketching the possibility that Harry Clifton may be one of the three sages whom Yeats discerned in the texture of his lapis lazuli stone? Perhaps, especially if the book the young woman on the train is reading is a book by Harry Clifton.

Here is what Yeats saw in that ten-and-a-half inches high tablet of lapis lazuli which Harry Clifton, son of Talbot and Violet Clifton, gave him for his seventieth birthday on 4 July 1935:

> Two Chinamen, behind them a third,
> Are carved in lapis lazuli,
> Over them flies a long-legged bird,
> A symbol of longevity;
> The third, doubtless a serving-man,
> Carries a musical instrument.

Perhaps we may also discern in the discolouration, cracks and dents of the three wise men of the Deux Magots as seen by Derek Mahon, the crouched, handsome figures of Benjamin Fondane and René Char. How well they knew one another one cannot be certain but in 1930s Paris they moved in the same circles. On 14 February 1930, Benjamin Fondane was sitting in the Bar Maldoror in Montparnasse when the bar was gate-crashed by André Breton accompanied by René Char, Louis Aragon, Paul Éluard and other surrealists who were protesting the commercial exploitation of the revered surrealist figure of the Count de Lautréamont. Fisticuffs may have ensued; certainly, according to Fondane's account, the women in the bar threw napkins at the aggressors.

Let us stroll down Boulevard Raspail from Montparnasse to the more sedate atmosphere of St Germain and, taking coffee in the Deux Magots, let us, by grace of the two blocks of lapis lazuli as depicted by W. B. Yeats and Derek Mahon, discern in their configurations the pro-files of Benjamin Fondane and René Char, two modern heroes who inspired two startling poems in the imaginative conscience of Harry Clifton, son of Charlie and Dorothy Clifton. If we do so, we may want to conclude that the face of the third carrying a musical instrument and 'doubtless a serving-man' is that of the same Harry Clifton who gave us these two redemption songs of the Vaucluse and of Auschwitz, two poems branded by an authenticity of primal fire as absolute as geological time, an authenticity which Clifton himself depicted in one of the first poems he ever published, 'Null Beauty':

I have a stone about me,
Round as I know round,
So without peculiarities
That I feel free

To imagine as I can,
Beyond the fact of stone,
A before and to come
It could never disclose
[...]
I can only rediscover it.
I can only make queries,
Draw what fire I can
From a cold, null beauty.

A transcript of a lecture given in University College Dublin, on 8 February 2007.

Paul Durcan was born in Dublin in 1944 and studied Archaeology and Medieval History at University College Cork. His first solo collection of poetry, *O Westport in the Light of Asia Minor*, won the Patrick Kavanagh Award in 1975; later collections include *Teresa's Bar* (1976), *Sam's Cross* (1978), *Ark of the North* (1982), *Jesus, Break His Fall* (1983), and *Going Home to Russia* (1987). *The Berlin Wall Café* (1985) was a choice of the London Poetry Book Society and *Daddy, Daddy* (1990) won the Whitbread Poetry Prize. Other publications include *Crazy About Women* (1991), *Give Me Your Hand* (1994), *Christmas Day* (1996), *Greetings to Our Friends in Brazil* (1999), *Cries of an Irish Caveman* (2001), *The Art of Life* (2004), *The Laughter of Mothers* (2007), *Life is a Dream: 40 Years Writing Poems 1967–2007* (2009), *Praise In Which I Live and Move and Have My Being* (2012), *The Days of Surprise* (2015) and *Wild, Wild Erie* (2016). Paul Durcan was the winner of the Lifetime Achievement Irish Book Award 2014. He is a member of Aosdána and lives in Dublin and Mayo. Paul Durcan was Ireland Professor of Poetry 2004–7.

ACKNOWLEDGEMENTS

The author and the publisher gratefully acknowledge the following for permission to reprint copyrighted material. Every effort has been made to seek copyright clearance on referenced text. If there are any omissions, UCD Press will be pleased to insert the appropriate acknowledgement in any subsequent printing or editions.

Harry Clifton: 'Death of Thomas Merton', from *Comparative Lives* (The Gallery Press, 1982); 'The Liberal Cage' and 'Vaucluse', from *The Liberal Cage* (The Gallery Press, 1988); 'Taking the Waters' and 'Watershed', from *Night Train through the Brenner* (The Gallery Press, 1994); 'Null Beauty' and 'Two Stations in Paris', from *The Walls of Carthage* (The Gallery Press, 1977). All reprinted by kind permission of The Gallery Press. 'Bare Arm', from *God in France* (Metre Editions, 2003). Reprinted by kind permission of Metre Editions. 'Benjamin Fondane Departs for the East', from *Secular Eden: Paris Notebooks 1994–2004* (Wake Forest University Press, 2007). Reprinted by kind permission of Wake Forest University Press.

Anthony Cronin: Sonnets 27, 30, 48, 49, 57, 74, 77, 92, 95, 102, 116, 131, 147, 149, 152, 159 and 179, from *The End of the Modern World*, from *Collected Poems* (New Island, 2004). Reprinted by kind permission of New Island.

Michael Hartnett: *Sibelius in Silence*, from *Collected Poems* (The Gallery Press, 2001) and 'Dán do Niall, 7/Poem to Niall, 7', from *A Necklace of Wrens* (The Gallery Press, 1987). Reprinted by kind permission of The Gallery Press.

Patrick Kavanagh: 'The Hospital', is reprinted by kind permission of the Trustees of the Estate of the late Katherine B. Kavanagh, through the Jonathan Williams Literary Agency.

Derek Mahon: 'Lapis Lazuli', from *Harbour Lights* (The Gallery Press, 2005). Reprinted by kind permission of The Gallery Press.

BIBLIOGRAPHY

Charles Baudelaire: 'Les Sept Vieillards', from *Charles Baudelaire: The Complete Poems*, translated by Walter Martin (Carcanet, 1997).

William Blake: *Milton*, from *Blake: The Complete Poems*, edited by W. H. Stevenson, second edition (Longman, 1989).

Robert Browning: 'Childe Roland', from *The Poems of Robert Browning*, volume III 1847–61, edited by John Woolford, Daniel Karlin and Joseph Phelan (Routledge, 2007).

David Burnett-James: *Sibelius* (Omnibus Press, 1989).

Mary Ann Caws: *René Char* (Twayne Publishers, 1977).

Harry Clifton: 'Bare Arm', from *God in France* (Metre Editions, 2003); 'Benjamin Fondane Departs for the East', from *Secular Eden: Paris Notebook 1994–2004* (Wake Forest University Press, 2007); 'Death of Thomas Merton', from *Comparative Lives* (The Gallery Press, 1982); 'Imaginative Absolute in Wallace Stevens', unpublished MA thesis, Department of Metaphysics, UCD, 1975; 'The Liberal Cage' and 'Vaucluse', from *The Liberal Cage* (The Gallery Press, 1988); 'Null Beauty' and 'Two Stations in Paris', from *The Walls of Carthage* (The Gallery Press, 1977); 'Shylock's lament', from *The Dublin Review* XVIII (spring 2005); and 'Taking the Waters' and 'Watershed', from *Night Train through the Brenner* (The Gallery Press, 1994).

John Cornford: 'Huesca', from *A Book of Love Poetry*, edited by Jon Stallworthy (Oxford University Press, 1973).

Hart Crane: 'The River', from *The Bridge* (Liveright, 1970).

Anthony Cronin: *The End of the Modern World*, from *Collected Poems* (New Island, 2004); foreword to *Selected Poems of James Clarence Mangan*, edited by Michael Smith (The Gallery Press, 1974); and *Samuel Beckett: The Last Modernist* (Flamingo, 1997).

Robert Duncan: 'A Poem Beginning with a Line by Pindar', from *Selected Poems*, edited by Robert J. Bertholf (New Directions, 1997).

T. S. Eliot: *The Waste Land* (Faber, 2013).

Benjamin Fondane: 'Métempsychose', from *Benjamin Fondane à la Recherche du Judaïsme* (Lethielleux, 2009) and 'Ulysses', from *Le Mal des Fantômes* (Verdier, 2006).

Michael Hartnett: 'Dán do Niall, 7/Poem to Niall, 7', from *A Necklace of Wrens* (The Gallery Press, 1987) and *Sibelius in Silence*, from *Collected Poems* (The Gallery Press, 2001).

Erich Heller: *The Disinherited Mind* (Penguin, 1961).

David Hume: *A Treatise of Human Nature*, edited by L. A. Selby-Bigge, second edition, revised by P. H. Nidditch (Clarendon Press, 1975).

Patrick Kavanagh: 'The Hospital', from *Collected Poems* (Penguin Classics, 2005).

Declan Kiberd: *The Field Day Anthology of Irish Writing*, volume III (W. W. Norton and Company, 1991).

Thomas Kinsella: 'Downstream', from *Downstream* (The Dolmen Press, 1962).

Robert Layton: *Sibelius* (J. M. Dent and Sons, 1965, revised edition 1992).

Deirdre Madden: letter, from *Lifelines 2*, edited by Niall MacMonagle (Townhouse, 1994).

Derek Mahon: 'Lapis Lazuli', from *Harbour Lights* (The Gallery Press, 2005).

Lazar Moscovici: *1942, Convoi No 8*, fourth edition (Editions du Retour, 2011).

Adolf Paul: *A Book about a Man* (Bonniers, 1891).

Edgar Allen Poe: *The Raven* (First Avenue Editions, 2014).

Ezra Pound: *The Pisan Cantos*, from *New Selected Poems and Translations*, edited by Richard Sieburth (New Directions, 2010) and 'The prose tradition in verse', from *Poetry* IV (1914).

Wallace Stevens: 'Esthétique du Mal', from *Collected Poems of Wallace Stevens* (Faber and Faber, 1955).

George Szirtes: 'Passionate in public', *Irish Times*, 18 December 2004.

Erik Tawaststjerna: *Sibelius*, 3 volumes, translated by Robert Layton (Faber, 1976, 1986, 1997).

Alfred Tennyson: 'Ulysses', from *Tennyson: A Selected Edition*, edited by Christopher Ricks (Pearse Education Ltd, 1969).

Colm Tóibín: *Martyrs and Metaphors* (Raven Arts Press, 1987).

Simone Weil: *Gravity and Grace* (Routledge and Kegan Paul, 1952).

W. B. Yeats: 'Lapis Lazuli', from *The Poems*, edited by Daniel Albright (J. M. Dent, 1992).

PUBLISHER'S NOTE

Some quotations attributed to Sibelius on p. 50 and 52 are from a short story by Julian Barnes about an unnamed composer who is undoubtedly Sibelius. See Julian Barnes: 'The Silence', from *The Lemon Table* (Jonathan Cape, 2004). On p. 50 Barnes is paraphrasing a famous quotation recorded in Cecil Gray's *Sibelius: The Symphonies* (Oxford University Press, 1935), p. 56, where Sibelius is quoted as having said: 'Whereas most other modern composers are engaged in manufacturing cocktails of every hue and description, I offer the public cold spring water.'